Crossing Twice:
Answers from the Source

Dr. Reece W. Manley, DD, M.Ed., MPM

Copyright © 2009 Dr. Reece W. Manley, DD, M.Ed., MPM. No part of this work may be reproduced or disseminated in any form or fashion, whether print or electronic means, without express written permission from the author.

Dr. Reece W Manley, DD, M.Ed., MPM, Rev.
A property of Advocate USA, LLC,

Foreword and Editing by: Freda Chaney, DD

Dedication

This work is dedicated to Dad, Mom, Ross, and Kerryann. You were there watching over me every second of my battle. You are the heroes in my life.

Contents

Foreword 5
Chapter One – My Death 9
Chapter Two - Lifepoints 13
Chapter Three - Out of the Veil And Into the Light 24
Chapter Four – The "Transfiguration" 28
Chapter Five – Finally Home 30
Chapter Seven – Joining the Source 32
Chapter Seven – The Return 44
Chapter Eight – Back to Life 49
Chapter Nine – Times Remembered 51
Chapter Ten – My Nemesis 52
Chapter Eleven - The Experience of Youth 58
Chapter Twelve – The Surgery 64
Chapter Thirteen – The Disability 68
Chapter Fourteen – The Acceptance of Chronic Pain 71
Chapter Fifteen – Surviving the Demon 77
Chapter Sixteen – Giving in to Depression 81
Chapter Seventeen – Before the Miracle 84
Chapter Eighteen – When I Crossed 89
Chapter Nineteen – Recovering from the Miracle 94
Chapter Twenty – Getting Beyond "Crazy" 100
Chapter Twenty One - The Journey Back 105
Chapter Twenty Two – Trauma Unit 110
Chapter Twenty Three – God in the Room 113
Chapter Twenty Four – Meeting the Chief 118
Chapter Twenty Five – "CPR! CPR!" 120
Chapter Twenty Six – When Hope Failed 125
Chapter Twenty Seven – The Business of Healing 130
Twenty-Eight – Where's the Spirit? 135
Chapter Twenty Nine - The Great Suzette Doescher 139
Chapter Thirty – Coming to Power 156

Chapter Thirty One - What I've Learned 159
Part Two 163
Ten Questions About my Journey to Heaven 163
Is Death Painful? 164
Do We See God? 166
What About Loved Ones Who Have Passed-On? 169
What Does Heaven Look Like? 171
What Do You Hear in Heaven? 174
How Do We Look in Heaven? 178
Are There Angels in Heaven? 181
Is There a Hell? 185
If We Go to Heaven, From Where Do We Come? 187
What Do We Do for All of Eternity? 188
Closing Remarks 191
Acknowledgements 194

Foreword

Dr. Reece Manley is a genuine, caring soul I found on PublishersMarketplace.com. At the time, we were both seeking an agent or publisher for spiritual books. I was at once intrigued by Dr. Manley's book title, **Crossing Twice: Answers from the Source.** Upon reading his Marketplace page, I learned that he is also a pastoral counselor with a string of degrees for clinical counseling and more. I decided to send him a note to wish him well on his book.

That began a correspondence that has benefited us both in many ways. Though we have not met face-to-face, we have shared many insightful conversations by mail. I was invited to edit his wonderful book. That work began an adventure for me, not only in learning the story of Dr. Reece Manley and his divine crossing-over during a near death experience, but also in discovering for myself that there were some challenges ahead for me in my own life story.

I was born in the Midwest, and have strong beliefs rooted in Christianity. Those beliefs were not instilled in me by my family, but by the Gideons who handed me a Bible at my little country school in the 1960s. Those Biblical views were mostly comforting, but could also be frightening for a young girl. I find that Dr. Manley has softened those views with his marvelously humble and insightful book, ***Crossing Twice: Answers from the Source.*** Your own views will be challenged as you read and grow within the covers of this fresh, spiritual look at life, and life after life!

Dr. Manley's story will amaze you. His struggle through high-level chronic pain is only one of many challenges he faces daily. Most of us cannot begin to imagine constant, high-level pain. Besides the chronic pain, there were other kinds of torment for Reece Manley—spiritual and emotional pain. Abuse by an uncle, left Dr. Manley emotionally scarred. One day after depleting his body with pain-killing substances, he crossed-over. That was the beginning of his spiritual healing. He learned, beyond the veil, that he was valued by God no matter who he was, or what he had done in his earthly life. Dr. Manley survived and thrived, and now shares what he learned to bless others daily in his counseling practice.

What Reece Manley offers from his remembrances in the presence of the Source, Spirit, Creator—however you relate to God, is convincing in a simple way like the teachings of Jesus. Christ's words still ring true today—that we need to LOVE one another because LOVE is of God. Jesus said that if we would humble ourselves like little children, we would be the greatest in the Kingdom of Heaven. If you think about it, the answer to the world's problems IS simple—the answer is LOVE. A childlike heart of humility, trust, compassion, and love will open new classroom doors no matter our ages, stations in life, or our religious, political, or professional affiliations.

If we allow ourselves to shake-off layers of dust, step forward on a new path of learning and discovery like small children holding wonder, then transformation is ours. If, instead, we remain entrenched in judgments of ourselves and others, and fail to apply LOVE, then we are stuck spiritually, and cannot free ourselves or bless others. The message of LOVE must first extend to YOU, the reader, and then out into a needy world. Dr. Manley's message will affect you in a profound way, opening doors to the Source of Love that he has seen, and now shares as a footpath for all. It's time for us to start walking toward that common footpath of the Lord for the sake of our survival on this planet.

Blessings,

Freda Chaney, D.D.

Crossing Twice:
Answers from the Source

Chapter One – My Death

Nothing happened to let me know I was dying. There I was, listening to the mechanical sounds of the ventilator, and hearing the murmur of loving voices. Peace enfolded me. There were no flashes of light. There were no bursts of joyous angel-song. It was calm, quiet, and gray. This is how my crossing over from life to death, from earth to heaven began.

The serene sounds had an effect on me. I felt better rested. I remember I tried to open my eyes. However, instead of my eyes opening, I simply became aware of a soothing gray mist.

The mist was everywhere, and I began to hear the rhythm of the ventilator fade, and the serenity expanded.

It was at this point I became aware that I was no longer in pain. The suffering had been so intense, and now there was none! The pain in my feet was the least of the physicians' concerns. The pain medication was being used very sparingly so as not to interfere with my respiration.

The sound of the ventilator began to fade in the background. I did not feel movement. It was as if things were simply fading away—fading away into this calm, gray mist. And there was no pain!

However, I still felt very much alive. I felt energy coursing through me. I felt as strong as I had ever been during my weight training sessions with my brother in the late 1980s. There was a pause—a moment.

And, then I was lifting weights with my brother! The first sensation was the smell. If you've ever been to a gym where the focus is on free weights you know the smell. There is an unmistakable odor that is a combination of sweat, disinfectant, and leather. I suddenly felt the leather gloves on my hands! The smell, the feel of gloves on my hands, and then – pop – my eyes were open, and I heard my brother cheering me on.

"Three man! You can do it! Now four!" came Ross' voice, much younger than it should have sounded. Along with the encouraging sound of Ross' voice, I felt the weight against my hands. I felt the intense load on my arms, and the muscles of my chest contracting. Another pop, audible pops this time like a speaker amplifier coming on. My sight improved, and I was, indeed, pushing-up a full load of weights in the middle of a bench press. My brother was standing above me, urging even more strongly to "push, push!" I could see the determination on his face, and I felt my pulse quickening. I wanted to make that "one more" before the whole bar come down on me!

The energy coursing through me doubled, and I let out a little laugh that came out more like a grunt. The noise surprised me. After all, I was in a hospital room in Texas in 2008, not in "The Gym", as they called it, circa 1989! But I was wrong about the hospital room. I was, indeed, in The Gym, and the only thing in the world that mattered was getting that weight up and onto the bar bench.

Next, suddenly, my taste buds were alive with flavor! I have no idea what I had eaten that day before I got to The Gym, but it was still lingering in my mouth! Another pop. The taste in my mouth was water. It all came together. I was in The Gym, sensing the smells, seeing my brother, hearing his voice, and tasting the swig of water I had taken from the water fountain a few moments before.

It was a point in my life when I had felt wonderful! I was strong and powerful. I was with the one person in my life in 1989 I would trust to lift weights off of me at just the right time. It also came to me that I was NOT going to get that weight up without Ross' help. I made another noise, and my brother smiled broadly and pretended to drop the bar toward me.

Then I heard, "Good job, Bro!" And the bar lifted up and into place. I jumped up from the bench, and clapped Ross on the shoulder. Ross took his place at the side of the weight bar, and began placing the weights back up on the rack. I was helping Ross when all of the sudden—pop!

Chapter Two - Lifepoints

Again there was no smell, no taste, no noise, no touch, and a serenity I can't describe. I was once again surrounded by the gray mist. I still felt energized, and I was feeling more so by the moment. I was feeling completely well, young, and strong. Yet, I was in the hospital—a thirty-nine-year-old body ravaged by MRSA Pneumonia, and the cumulative years of neuropathy pain, sometimes so severe that walking was impossible! How could this be? How could I be this sickened body in the hospital bed, and at the same time, by all appearances, this virile young man lifting weights with my brother?

Ross remained in my thoughts deep in that gray mist, but no longer did I experience him as I had moments before. Then—pop!

I felt the warmth of sunlight on my skin. It was one of those ethereal moments when you really feel something as though for the first time. Then, my eyes saw the sunlight. The gray had faded away, and I was in glorious beams of sunlight! Next, in the back of my mouth a taste presented itself—a fruit, something ambrosial—not a fruit I had everyday. Tropical! Yet another, pop, and a spark, and my mouth was flooded with the taste of pineapple. And not just pineapple, but a mixture containing coconut and the smooth burn of rum. I was in the sunlight, and drinking a pina colada! Now this was getting a bit closer to heaven! I was still very energized. I felt so incredibly good, so incredibly strong. My thoughts began, "Rian, that looks great! Now try some blue." My eyes were suddenly reporting right along with my thoughts, and I was sitting outside by a pool at a Mexican resort. Somewhere in either Cancun or Playa del Carmen.

Rian is my eight-year-old nephew. That day, I had the honor of being the center of his attention for a few moments. He was dutifully painting in the activities area outside by the pool. I looked over at him, and he grinned and nodded as he admired his work and reached for the blue.

The shade of blue was that beautiful hue of cerulean that can only be found in the Caribbean Sea, and it existed as only a small thin line of the brilliant hues going from the white sand to the deep navy of the open sea. *How did the staff manage to find that blue, and place it in a bottle to paint one of their souvenirs?* Rian grabbed the brush and dabbed the ceramic plate with the color. The next smell came to me on the fresh breezes whipping around us. It was paint. I have never experienced the smell of paint so completely! Oh, I am quite familiar with paint, but not this intensity—this brightness of smell. Forgive my Martha Stewart explanation, but it smelled fresh, clean, with a hint of earthiness.

Rian continued his painting as I leveled my gaze to the ocean, and swallowed the taste of the frozen concoction in my mouth. I looked down again at the table, and was aware of everything in the scene. The newspapers were spread-out to catch the drips of paint. Rian was an enthusiastic painter, and there were several splotches of excess paint on the newspaper. A cup full of water was holding a brush in place; streaks of red tinted the hairs from a previous application. I was lost in the scene, and pondered what it would be like to be young again—like Rian.

Pop.

The sunlight still beamed, but this time it was staving-off a cool wind. The little boy with me was much younger than Rian. It was a different boy! I was with my brother, Ross again. Only this time, he was three or four years old, and I could tell I wasn't much older. There were adults talking next to us as we walked past them on the way to see the ducks. Ducks! What wonderful creatures were these huge, orange-legged ducks! Ross and I were out with our mom, clutching fists full of stale bread, and seeking-out the greatest thing in the world—ducks! Ross pronounced the word differently. Dlucks! "Dlucks, Leece! Dlucks, Momma!" I understood my little brother perfectly, and I called to Mom. "We're coming, Momma. Where are the ducks?" My voice sounded young too. The lady I called to was a tall, pretty lady, and when she turned, I knew she was Momma. Momma, Ross, and I were feeding the ducks on a perfect day full of sunshine and cool winds!

Pop.

I was running at high speed toward a body of water. But instead of ducks, I was sneaking-up on an old girlfriend with every intention of knocking her into the pool before she noticed me. My friend, Ron, was there and wearing his impish, sly smile he reserved for occasions such as this. My very good friend, Ron, was indeed right there! He was wearing red swim trunks, and pulling-off the kind of "cool" that only sixteen-year-old guys can pull-off! Then, my hands made contact with the softest thing I had ever felt: the skin of my girlfriend. She screamed wildly as I held her, and carried us both into the water. The waves were cold, and she was hanging on to me for dear life. Then, again, pop!

So cold, so very, very cold! Instead of sunlight, we had gray skies, but it didn't seem to matter. We were together—my girlfriend and I were getting-up from an overturned snowmobile I had managed to run into a tree at Red River. I was seventeen, and driving the snowmobile. The instructor had told us to lean together, and when I leaned left, she leaned right, and the tree stood still! It was funny, in the way all things seem funny to two young people exploring love. As we laughed, I could taste the snow in my mouth. At that moment, plain snow seemed delightful on my tongue. It was so pristine, so wonderfully clean. Our sides were hurting from laughing so hard. I scooped her up, and headed down the mountain. She was the lightest thing in the world, and she was safe in my arms, safe from the elements, safe from the snowmobile. I enjoyed making her safe. I was her hero. I was feeling so proud of myself for saving my lady from danger! Then, pop!

I was still feeling very proud when I plunged a fat little hand into a man's face, saying the words, "Pay up!" It took a minute for me to figure out where I was when I heard my voice speak. The voice was immature. My hand held the latest report card from Ms. Garcia's sixth grade class. It was full of As from top to bottom except for Physical Education. The smile across my daddy's face was thick with whiskers as he dutifully studied the report card. The smell of his cigar filled the air—a smell so immediately familiar, then – pop!

It was New Year's Eve, and my family and I were on our first cruise. Dad was smoking his cigar on the deck, and complaining about smoking restrictions. He could only smoke on deck, or in the casino. Suddenly, my head began to swim, and my mouth tasted of champagne! My eyes focused on my sister-in-law who was wearing the most beautiful shimmering dress. The wind was blowing against it, leaving the impression of her body, like a mermaid. We were on our first trip, using the "new" money my fathers and brother's business had earned. Dad and his wife were laughing, but I couldn't focus enough to see them. Then, I saw the stars reaching out so far into the heavens! The ship's lights paled in comparison.

The pops would continue for another twenty or thirty times. Each time I shifted, I was awestruck by the reality of the scene in which I found myself. Every one of the human senses was involved sharply and completely as the scenes changed. It seemed to occur in the order of: smell, sight, touch, sound, and then taste.

I have no doubt whatsoever that I was actually revisiting these times in my life. I was not simply reviewing them, or remembering them. I was there again! It seems impossible, but it held true for each session. There was no dream-like quality. It was sharp. It was in focus. I learned about half-way through the experiences that I was consciously able to will myself, by simple memory, into the moment of the events!

I did not visit any of the darker times of my life. I don't know if I would have been able to do so even if I had tried. But the gloriousness of the experience was so overwhelming that I thought I had found "Heaven"! I could go back and enjoy the full experience of moments I had lived in my human body on earth.

As I recall these things, tears stream down my cheeks. Those moments in time were perfect for the time in which they were lived. However, today in full life context, the scenes do not connect in such happy ways. Dear friends I revisited during those crossing moments are lost to me now through my carelessness of not keeping in touch with them. Sad moments would follow many of the happy ones on the paths I had revisited. Nevertheless, to be able to visit just those precise moments, without having them relate to all the other less desirable moments in my life, was delightful.

Each memory was picture-perfect! My relationships to those in the memories were exactly as they should have been for those moments. I wept. There was a deep sadness. I missed the relationships—now long lost. Time had taken me from their good graces, or them from mine, depending on the point of view. But, I loved them all dearly! I will close this remembrance with one of the strongest experiences I had.

Pop – I was walking home as hard as I could—a fat, twelve-year-old, fifth grader in a very small west Texas town. It was a dusty spring day. Dirt hung in the air, the way it does outside of Lubbock, Texas. I was wheezing from the dust and heat. The whirr of the cotton gin was purring out the sound of area commerce. My body was heavy over the little round legs carrying it. A tear escaped down my cheek. One more block. One more block, and I would arrive at my Grannie V's house. I can clearly smell the grass and cotton dust in the air. Wheezing and puffing, I trudged up the slope between the streets, down three more houses, and left into Grannie V's house. There she was, seated in the living room.

I had had a bad day. One of my schoolmates had called me "lard butt." I had had another asthma attack, and couldn't play outside with the other kids. Just a generally bad day! However, as soon as I walked into the front door, that was all behind me. There in her white cloth chair, as though seated on a cloud, was my Grannie V. I can still smell her wonderful scent. It was a combination of bath powder and cooking scents that even today smells like "home" to me. She stood up, and asked me what was wrong. I started to explain, but it all came out as garbled sounds, and then I began to cry. I have shed some tears in my life, but this one was one of the big ones.

She put her big, soft arms around me, and held me close. I smothered her polyester pantsuit jacket in large tears and sweat. I tried to catch my breath, but only managed gasps in between the cries. Then she started crying and cooing, "Now, Reece, you just calm down, Sweetheart." The sound of her sweet voice made me cry even harder. Now, I could even feel the flush in my cheeks from crying and struggling to breathe. She held me, and let me cry, all the while rocking me, and singing a familiar rock-a-bye tune. From the scratchy feel of her jacket, to the smell of her hairspray, it was one of the best hugs I would have for years! Many years later, I would cry on a shoulder at my hospital bed in a scratchy jacket and think of her. But for now, for that relived moment in time when I was twelve, and safe in my Grannie V's arms, the cry was sweet release. I was safe, in for the day, at rest, and the world was going to be okay. I was going to be OK! My Grannie V told me so, and I believed her.

Pop.

Chapter Three - Out of the Veil And Into the Light

There came a time when I knew the moment was right to end my flash reviews of life. The scene on the last "pop" stayed gray rather than fading into another sensation of sight. If taste could be gray, it would have been just the same—that lackluster nothingness—a veil thrown over a scene. The silence was stifling. No longer was there a scent in my nostrils, and I'd lost the sense of touch. I suddenly found myself without any feedback at all from my body. Even my mind was empty. Empty, gray, and extending in every direction! Alternatively, was it extending at all? I'll never be sure what to call that state of being. I went from being corporeal to being air-like. I seemed a whisper in the great cause of things. And then came the Light!

The Light was overwhelmingly beautiful! It did not fade in, it burst in! It was a symphony of light, as if dapples of sunlight on a pond's surface were transforming into the full brilliance of the sun. It wasn't just white and continuous; it streamed around me, through me, above me, and below me. My mind came back into being. I finally could begin to gather words to describe what was happening. For a few moments, I had been without any form, or any senses of any kind in the presence of the great Light. Now that I was beginning to gather what was happening around me, I was even more overwhelmed.

Overwhelmed! The word is not sufficient to describe the emotions running through me as I began to finally see, and not just sense the scene. As the Light filled my eyes with a thousand degrees of bright, the first heavenly emotions began to warm my heart.

The emotions came slowly at first. Love. Incredible love, the depth of which I could only begin to fathom, surrounded me. It was as is if it were both emotion and motion, coming from the inside, and swimming around the outside of me. It pulsed in my mind, and my soul seemed to sing. The Love was so large, so great, and so infinite that to stand in it was like standing as a child on the edge of the ocean.

Love was a part of the great Light, and as I tried to reconcile these two great concepts of Love and Light in my limiting mind, I began to do the things we humans do in the face of love. I laughed so loud, I thought the very heavens were resounding with sound of my happiness. Then, tears fell in deep appreciation of the depth of this Love. How great was this Love, and it was directed at me! This unquestionably infinite Love was directed at me! I! I—who had never done anything worthy of being totally loved in my whole life! I drew in a breath. I was aware I was breathing in the Light and the Love, and exhaling it as well! Unaffected by physical rules, I felt myself being lifted-up—weightless in the presence of the Love and the Light.

Here, today, as I write this, I smile without effort, knowing that kind of Love exists—that kind of Light exists. And this was just the beginning of knowing the "face" of God. Light and Love, Love and Light swirling around inside of me, outside of me, and through me, all at the same time!

I have heard stories of deaf people who undergo surgery, and were able to recover their hearing. One of the challenges the recovery presents, is the "noise" of hearing. It can be so unusual to hear, that the brain can't comprehend anything other than a big blast of gibberish. The patients have to pace how they introduce sound to their brains, so they can adjust the sound level to comprehendible segments of communication. It takes quite a bit of work to go from deafness to hearing, beyond just the flip of a switch.

So it was with this Love and this Light. I had been as a deaf man suddenly listening to Beethoven blasting at 300 decibels! But as I adjusted to the Light and the Love, I became steadily more aware of my surroundings. Instead of just one loud note of Love, it was a symphony or choir tuned and practiced to perfection. In it, I began to see and feel different notes. It was still as powerful and just as bright, but I was applying some understanding about what was happening. A shape was beginning to form, and my mind worked to comprehend what it was, where I was at, and what was going on around me!

Chapter Four – The "Transfiguration"

I was standing on the edge of a cliff, the bottom of which could not be seen. It was incredibly deep. Above me, the heavens stretched-out beyond infinity. In front of me, taking up almost my entire field of vision, but still what seemed thousands of miles away, the great Light shimmered. The Light, I knew, was the infinite Love of God. It was warm, soft, and glowing around me.

I started to notice the edges of the Light, and how they were continually shifting, expanding, and contracting ever so slightly. The Light was streaming-out in wide channels, and beginning to coalesce into rays coming from the main Light. It was still blinding, but was taking shape as a sphere—a brilliant sun. The surface of the Light rippled and danced with small ridges rising-up and down like waves on the face of a lake.

The rays coming out of the Light were emanating into other spheres of Light. As my eyes adjusted to the scene, I could see thousands and thousands, perhaps billions of these smaller spheres connected by a channel of Light to the great Light. As the great Light pulsed, the smaller spheres would pulse in joyous response.

It had ceased to be quiet in my experience of this great Light. In fact, the air was alive with praises. The sound was sweeter than any hymn I had ever heard, and as the smaller spheres pulsed along with the great Light, the sound became sweeter still. The love was palpable. Along with the love, was a sense of acceptance and belonging, which I had never felt. One word began to form in my mind, and that word was "home." I was home! My salvation through the Love of Christ had brought me home. The definitions of home change from culture to culture, from place-to-place, and over time. It has been my experience in life, that very few people describe home as being simply a physical space. I do know of a few very lonely, lost people who have worked hard to earn enough money to buy a home—a home made of wood, brick, and mortar. They had laid the best marble, and the finest granite to make the home aesthetically-pleasing, but in truth, they are just houses.

Chapter Five – Finally Home

Some of my favorite earthly homes have been very simple. My early childhood in Texas was spent in a very humble dwelling that I considered a "mansion." One of the best homes I ever had was a small wood frame farmhouse, which was always dusty from the cotton fields. It was in desperate need of painting, and the kitchen had a slope in the floor big enough to cause the refrigerator door to swing open at a wide-angle when the handle was released. But again, these were just "houses." What made them home was the love, care, and acceptance found within those walls. Safety came in hugs and laughter, and sharing was evident at meals. Yes, I feel very sorry for those who don't know the difference between going to a house and going "home."

Visiting there in our heavenly home, I was very aware there were no golden streets, or great mansions. But it was the most incredible home I had ever visited! The Father was there in the great Light. Siblings were among the thousands of smaller spheres, and there was room enough for all.

Some who have read Christ's words, may take them to mean there are literal walls, houses, and mansions in His Father's realm. In my own experience, there was no proof of dwellings. I saw no houses, or mansions, or walls.

There were many other smaller spheres linked to the great Light of the Father. I became aware that even though I was thinking like a human being, I no longer resembled a human. I had joined the others, and had become a sphere of light. It is hard to explain exactly "what" I was, or how much space I possessed. But like so many things during the time of the crossing, I just knew.

Coming to know that I was a little dazzlingly bright sphere, reflecting the Light of the Father, took some time to sink-in. I just remained still, and enjoyed the sights and sounds, and the wonderful love and acceptance. That alone would have satisfied me for an eternity. But heaven didn't stop there for me. In fact, it was only the beginning!

Chapter Seven – Joining the Source

I mentioned earlier that the channels of Light entered into each of the little spheres, and connected them to the great Light. It wasn't long before I realized that the spheres were One—all connected to the great Light. I received my very own "rope" to the main Light! A little string, at first, connecting the Father and me, began to form. I was "plugged in" to God! Talk about a lifeline! I was filled instantly with God's love and compassion. I realized how wrong I had been in life to have ever judged or limited God's power. God's love has no limits! That I was getting a direct plug-in to this Truth, was an incredible eye-opener. If you can imagine how a single Christmas light would react being directly connected to the outlet, rather than to a full string, you might find an apt example of how I was sensing that event. Zap! Bing! I was filled with the Light. I became aware there were not only strings going from the great Light to the smaller lights, but there were strings connecting all the lights!

As soon as I "saw" this phenomenon, I became aware that the Holy Spirit is the "String" that attaches us all to the Father, and to each other. Suddenly, I knew each of the other spheres immediately and completely.

It is, of course, beyond my ability to comprehend that connection now. But, there, in my Father's home, I became aware of a great multitude of lives. And each of the Lights knew me! When I use the word "knew," I am again limited to our vocabulary. I also knew each of them intimately and immediately. I knew the soul of a woman who had lived to be 113. I knew the soul of a child who had died at the age of four in a drowning accident. I knew a deceased husband eagerly awaiting the arrival of his wife. There were inventors, scientists, philosophers, preachers, sinners, saints, and sewer workers. Within God's home, there were lives from all backgrounds throughout the eons of time. Some of the lights were new arrivals, and were being greeted at that time by loved ones on the other side. Soon, those who loved and knew me in Heaven, as well as those who knew me in my earth life, would greet me!

Before I begin that recount, I want to say a word about the angels I saw. Flights and flights of angels were around the Heavens. Some were in flight in full bodies as we have imagined them. Others were little Lights, without the ropes to any of us "humans," but they were connected to the Father. Unlike all of us, moving and dancing and shimmering to the light, the angels moved purposefully, and separately from any of us. Truly, we humans seemed to have our feet propped-up, while the angels were hard at work! They moved in-and-out of the edge of the great Light, and back-and-forth through the veil. Yes, there are, indeed, angels, and they are different from human beings! They are very, very busy creatures. Judging from what I saw, there were plenty of them to go around for each human life.

"Struck" is a good word for the next thing I experienced. It is also one of the most frustrating parts of the experience because I was back to work with the limitations of a human mind. You see, as I saw my string become a rope, and connect into the great Light, and out into the other Lights, I suddenly became aware of all knowledge. The complete history of Pakistan was there, right down to the memories of those who had first settled the lands! Calculus, a field I never mastered, was suddenly child's play to me! I knew all there was to know of history, sociology, psychology, theology, biology, and every other –ology! There was literally nothing, or no one I did not know. Any question my mind could form was quickly answered with an inflow of information. Dates of events, great and small, were known to me, as were the people and places involved. I would like to say more about this topic, but I fear it would be divisive between the truth I know from this experience, and the truth offered by many of today's churches. Let me just say that while in Heaven, I met a wife who had loved me, and still loved me. However, in my earth life, I had never been married!

After the knowledge, then came the feelings. The emotions and world views of everyone in the Light were instantaneously known to me. Of all the emotions clamoring for my attention, one thing came through above all else: Love. I was receiving virtual hugs, and I knew that I was known to everyone and loved by everyone. I reveled in this love for awhile. This love was the kind that people search for their entire lives. Yet, those on the other side had more love than could be imagined or expressed. The love was everywhere, and it was impossible to take too much. It was an endless supply of the very thing I had needed in my human life. Instead of having to search for the kind of love described in the Bible (I Corinthians 13), one could not keep from being caught up and swept away by the love!

As love came into me, it had a physical sensation. It was as though I was being filled with a warm fluid. My being filled up, and then the love quickly began to flow from me through the cord between the great Light and myself. It was filling me, and then accepting back the overflow with my little contribution added to it!

Joy owned my emotions. Joy is so much more than just happiness. Joy is an abiding emotion rather than the fleeting feeling of happiness. Happiness is our emotions reacting to a short-term situation. However, joy is a long-term condition, usually obtained through faith and prayer. Joy lasts through life's challenges. It brings with it a sense of calm and fulfillment—a sense of knowing that you are in the hands of the Father. I thought I knew the meaning—the feeling of joy on earth, but I'd fought for that sensation. Having battled chronic pain for almost eight years, I had found calm, and a quiet acceptance. But, this joy—this crossing over experience, was something I had never felt or even imagined. It was my total fulfillment of expectations. Here, joy was as available as air. Not only was it available, it was being piped through the cord of Light.

The cord was growing! As I noticed my physical form, I noticed I was no longer the shape of a human! I was a golden shimmering sphere! I pulsed and danced, and flew through the other Lights who were present in the space around the great Light. I had no hands, but I could feel the Light! I was free to move about, but my cord was tied to the Light at all times. I could easily will myself to move closer to the other Lights, or approach the great Light. Although I had no ears, I could hear the sounds of the Light. A great chorus sang praises of joy and love. The words came in all languages, but my mind easily understood the sounds regardless of the tongues that they were singing! Again, I was baffled by the amount of knowledge I had, including the ability to understand, and speak all languages instantly!

I had studied Greek in college. However, here, I easily understood French as well, and Russian came to me easily. Italian seemed a natural language to me. Amy Grant once sang, about love being understood in any language. I have to wonder where she got this insight, because in Heaven, there are no language barriers. Every word that passed through my mind made perfect sense.

As I began to become accustomed to the streams of knowledge passing through me via my line of light to the great Light, I somehow managed to think about questions in my earth life for which I had wanted answers. The way to ask such questions came naturally.

"Father, what happened during my surgery to damage my nerves?" The question flowed-out from me in a quick pulse. A second later, another pulse came down from the great Light as coming from a Physician. "During the procedure, myelin sheaths are especially vulnerable to...," the answer continued completely, satisfying my curiosity, but beyond what my mind now can fully recall.

"Father, what causes ALS, and how can it be cured?" My line pulsed to the great Light. A pulse brought back an answer. I saw it in its childlike simplicity. I can no longer recall that response. Then my questions moved from the physical to the philosophical.

"Father, what is our purpose on the earth?" A pulse out. A pause. A pulse back with the most beautiful answer. This time, however, I had an anchor to hang the answers on. The words I received were contained in the Bible—the Bible that existed before man had changed it?!

"Father, why do you not heal me?" A pulse returned. Again, there were answers that seemed so simple. Again, I had the benefit of being able to hang the answer on verses in the Bible so I could remember them.

"Father, when will the earth end?" Another pulse, sent through the Father, explained the end of the earth, but not the end of mankind! The math equations and the science involved are beyond our abilities here, but there in the presence of God, it was child's play.

As many of us would when given the opportunity, I asked many questions. Some of great importance, others of significance to only a very few. I sent and received books of answers through the Light of the Father.

The more I interacted with the Father, the more I knew I was in His Kingdom. Soon, more of those who had gone before came to see me, and to exchange love and joy with me. This included some of the people I never knew I had influenced on the earth plane. But when they saw me, their energy was ecstatic about being in my presence again. One of the first to come to me, and exchange love, laughter, and history, was my old girlfriend's father, Rob. He had always been a trickster, and was well known in his small town for being "larger than life." All were devastated when he died of a heart attack in his early fifties. Rob came to me, and I immediately knew him, especially by his laugh. I recounted the times I had spent with him and his daughter.

Next, a beloved friend who had died with AIDS, pulsed and danced over to me. He was much like I had known him in life. Bubbly, loving, vivacious, and dazzling. He had found love and peace in the Light that he had never known on earth. His life had taken him from one relationship to another trying to find genuine love—someone who would love him for more than just his body. It was not to happen during his life, but at last, he had found that love on the other side! In the Light of the Father, he had been made whole.

Some will be angry that I did not include Hell in these remembrances. After all, if there is no Hell, why are we trying so hard? Why you are trying so hard is between you and God. No one can change the way you limit your relationship with God except you.

There was the semblance of what I would call Hell. There were "energies" on the other side that represented lives that were not linked to the Light. Selfish and fearful, they were full of hate to the point of refusing to accept the overwhelming Love—God. They stayed dark and unconnected, and moved among all of us with no recognition of those around them. Like stones in a river, they were isolated, alone, dark, and quickly forgotten. We, who were connected, passed them by in our dance of love and joy with the Light.

As my time continued in the Light, I noticed my connection became larger and larger. The feelings of love, joy, and peace continued to increase beyond anything humans can conceptualize or describe. My connection, again, was not just with the Light of the Father, but through the Father, through the Holy Spirit. I was connected to all who were in the Light. While I was there, I became aware of everyone. It seems impossible to be connected intimately to unknown numbers of souls, but yet it was what was happening. Intimate details were known to me, running the gamut from where they were born, to what they had done in life, and were doing now on the other side. I had only to focus on one spirit, and I was immediately in connection with it. The parade of people I had known continued. One of the last ones I experienced was my Uncle Wayne.

Uncle Wayne had passed with ALS. It had been a horrible death. He had been a strong man—a farmer who had worked hard all of his life. He was a pillar in his community, but when he was stricken with Lou Gehrig's disease, he became a weakened visage of his former self. It affected every nerve in his body, leaving him less and less powerful. When he passed, he was in horrible pain, and his body was twisted beyond recognition. But how wonderful Uncle Wayne appeared in Heaven! His sphere of Light was bright and healthy. He was full of joy and peace. He embraced me through the Light, and it was a wonderful, strong hug like the ones he had given me as a child. This was my Uncle Wayne as I remembered him—as God created him, and intended him to be for eternity.

Chapter Seven – The Return

I was floating high on the love and joy, singing in my soul of the peace and acceptance I was experiencing. I was so happy. I was out of pain. And, most importantly, I was home. I knew I had many people yet to see, especially Grannie V.

Then it happened! I saw the one woman in my life that had taught me about unconditional love. Other than my mother, I was closer to no other woman while I had been alive. Grannie V had loved me deeply, and had always supported me no matter what I did. I remember my call to preach, and how she had enthusiastically adopted the idea. She pushed me forward in love and joy. Of course, I had had other aspirations while growing-up, and she stood behind every one.

Grannie V had a special talent for making a child feel as if he were the only person in the world at any given moment. She wasn't perfect, but she was as close as one could get on earth.

Here, she was perfect! She had the same robust, extra bright Light I'd seen around my Uncle Wayne. They both had lived challenging lives, but never lost faith. They continued to find joy, believed in love, and prayed to their Father in heaven, even in their darkest moments on earth.

I am not suggesting their reward was any greater than any other soul in the Light, but they were bright, beaming Lights! I was delighted to sense my Grannie V. I could not wait to exchange thoughts and love with her. This wonderful, wonderful woman from my past was alive and well. And she was here with me!

Suddenly, I sensed confusion. I felt concern from her, and a resistance. It was as if she had a terrible secret to share. And she did. First she exchanged a "hug" with me. Hugs in heaven are wonderful, powerful celebrations in the Light. They are explosions of joy! I have received wonderful hugs here on the earth, but to have one in Heaven is a life-altering experience. You are surrounded by joy through an ecstatic exchange of the essence of the other person. I was going to love my life in the Light!

That is when my confusion turned to terror. My Grannie V had simple words to say, "I love you, Reece. Even so, it is not your time. Your path is not complete. You will see us again. Back where you are going, it will seem a very long time until your return here. However, to us, it will only be a moment.

I am proud of you. Go back and do the things you need to do."

My thoughts screamed, "No!" I had just come from the ICU where my body lay full of illness and tubes. My feet were on fire with pain at all times. I suffered from depression. I did not want to go back!

Pop. Buzz. Pop!

I was going back. I felt as if I were falling. The great channel of Light and Love that had developed between the Father, and I began to shrink in size. It went from being as thick as a tree trunk to the diameter of a rope. Falling away! The sound, which seconds before had been a joyous chorus, became a babbling confusion of noise. It was full of clashing dialects and sounds. I no longer understood the many, many languages I'd "learned" instantly in the Light. My mind tried to hold on to the information I had received. The advanced words from beyond: "myelin sheath and neurochemical reagents," faded, and were replaced by the limits of my human knowledge. What was it I had heard in the Light? What was it I had received? My wife! What wife? The more I fell, the less I could recall certain knowledge about my excursion to Heaven. Pop.

It was dark. My first sensation was the smell of the hospital room. The odor of antiseptic, and the acrid smell of body fluids stung my nasal cavities. I was not alone—a medical team was there, and a tube was being pulled out of my nose. My feet began to sting and burn. No, no, no! I did not want to be back! The pain and the illness were too much to bear. I had crossed-over to the Light; what could I have done to deserve to be returned to this inhumane level of pain? But back I was, and I tried to form words to communicate what had just happened to me. My mouth would only form guttural sounds. Tears fell freely.

One of the nurses stopped long enough to squeeze my hand. "Getting that tube out is never fun, Baby, but you are back with us, so it's got to come out!"

I shut my eyes tightly, trying to remember everything. I could recall sketches of the experiences, which I have recorded here. I was back. The team was gone, and I was alone in the ICU room. It seems as though I cried for hours.

Chapter Eight – Back to Life

The entire hospital stay lasted for months! I had been admitted because I had basically given up on life. I know that sounds like a horrible thing to say after sharing my story. However, I had grown so tired of the pain, and the way it had taken me down.

Those who have never experienced it, can't easily understand chronic pain. Everyone understands what happens when you break an arm, or scrape a knee. That is a brief physiological sensation that lasts a few hours. Most people are able to diminish it with a Tylenol or an aspirin. Sometimes it may take a few days of codeine-based drugs. Nevertheless, it is a temporary pain that can be managed. Chronic pain is with you every day of your life. Every minute. Every second. Year after year. If you are someone who has experienced chronic pain, then you may begin to understand the choices I made which landed me in the hospital that December day. I had been medicating with alcohol. Medicating liberally and with great abandon. No doctor would prescribe a month of intoxication as a course of treatment, but that was the cure I tried. My body disagreed with me. More specifically, my liver had disagreed. I remember the concerned nurse's words, "He's being admitted for jaundice."

That was the tenuous situation I was in when I arrived at the hospital, and I quickly went downhill from there. I learned much later, that I had become seriously ill. I had longed for death, and suddenly I was that close, not intentionally opening the door, but the door was opened!

Chapter Nine – Times Remembered

In order to understand how very defeated I felt my life had become, you'll need to know a bit about me, and the trials I had faced in my life. This is a rather unhappy part of my journey, but I think I need to say a few words about it. I expect no pity. Pity never helps. However, some understanding is required to "see" the roots of emotional pain. For that reason, I share the rest of my story.

Growing up is difficult. I think it is, in one way or another, for all children. Even so, in my case, as in a percentage of many childhood cases, I had some special challenges. I had an uncle named Tom who was the main nemesis of my childhood. He was the eldest son in my mother's family. Their parents, I knew lovingly as Pa and Grannie V.

Pa and Grannie V had a wonderful daughter in my mother. She was a little girl full of strength, hope, and fun. She became the apple of my Grannie V's eye, and their relationship was strong, though full of ups and downs. Following next in age in the family came my uncle Tom. He did not have an easy life from the very beginning, even in his younger years.

Chapter Ten – My Nemesis

Tom was born with cystic fibrosis. Some doctors during that time thought it would be best not to allow a child with such challenges to live. However, to my Fundamentalist grandparents, there was no choice but to embrace the child. Tom's illness soon became the focus of the family. Even with the birth of their other sons, my Pa and Grannie V's energies focused on Tommy and his needs as the horrible disease advanced.

Many of the memories of mom's childhood were centered on family trips to take Tommy to one specialist, then another. Financial resources were scarce as my grandfather scratched out a simple living growing cotton in the unpredictable west Texas weather and soil. However, harvest would always come, and some money would be available.

Being good parents, Grannie V and Pa tried to help Tommy. Grannie V loved him deeply, and suffered along with Tom.

Suffice it to say they were doing the best they could with the limited resources they had.

My mother suffered through a hard childhood of her own. Then she met my father in high school. Mom was pretty and smart, the pride of Grannie V. She won the heart of my father, and they were soon dating. They married, and several years later, I arrived. When I came onto the scene, I was a "first" in many ways. I was Grannie V and Pa's first grandchild. I was my paternal grandparents' first grandson. I was my mother's first child. I was a happy baby in the spotlight.

Tommy had already progressed into a dark place with his disease. He had become bitter and angry, and trouble was brewing beneath the surface. He was a prisoner to the disease that severely limited his life. He took breathing treatments many times a day. He could not hold down a job, or have a relationship. The illness seemed to block him at every turn, and he had given in to its isolation and insidious nature.

My arrival did not sit well with Tommy. He had been the center of attention all of his life. He had learned the role of a victim, and had given it his full energy. Everything had been about Tommy. Suddenly, he had competition from a wriggling, happy, healthy boy, named Reece. My Grannie V would make a fuss over me at every opportunity. Mother, too, gave me her full attention. She had become a surrogate parent to Tommy, but now she had her own child, and Tommy's needs had to take second place. Tommy's hate for me increased. He was jealous and angry, and would soon make me a target. I will only mention part of one incident of his abuse, and I will tell it from a child's perspective. You may wish to skip the rest of this chapter if you would prefer not to read this part of my story.

It was Easter Sunday. I was eight years old. I had become a rather plump kid who turned to food to handle my emotions at the well-intentioned advice of my Grannie V. Nothing, after all, was so bad that it couldn't be overcome with a fine meal of fried chicken, mashed potatoes, and a pie made from scratch! To this day, I still find a nice friend in a chocolate cake!

I was dressed in my new Easter clothes. Regardless of the budget crisis of the moment, either my mom or my Grannie V would see that my brother and I had new clothes for church. After all, it was a family show-off day!

I can't remember everything, but I do remember how I ended up in my Uncle Tom's trailer, which was located on my Grannie V and Pa's property. They had hoped that giving Tom his own place would encourage him to be more active in life. Tommy was not tidy, and consequently, there were odors in the trailer that repulsed me. I never felt safe there in many ways.

On this particular Easter day, Uncle Tom told me that the best Easter egg was in his trailer. Whether it contained money or chocolate, I didn't care, I was definitely interested in getting the best Easter egg! I wanted bragging rights over my brother and my cousins who were gathered there for the Easter celebration. I had followed Tom back to his trailer, and once inside, he locked the door. He had never done that before, but I was still focused on the idea of that prize egg.

"Come here and sit on my lap, and I will tell you where it is," my Uncle Tom said. These words still echo in my mind with slurred reverberations. Uncle Tom had made sitting on his lap an activity of late, and one I knew I didn't like. But, the call of the prize egg was great. I responded to the request, and sat on his lap. A few seconds later, through a terrible display of strength, my Uncle Tom ended my childhood as I had known it. The rip of the pain terrified me. Tom became cruel, and he growled his words, "Shut up! I'll tell them all if you don't shut up! They'll know how weird you are. They'll know, and they'll hate you!" The words, "They'll hate you," still ring as an eerie echo in my memories. Even now, it seems as if I could lift my head and hear the same words out loud. It didn't last long, the pain subsided, and I started crying. I didn't know what else to do, but cry.

I was eight, my clothes had been pulled apart, my body reverberated in pain, my mind filled with fear, and I simply cried and cried. Uncle Tom's voice returned to normal as he cooed how much he loved me, and how special I was to him. He handed me a five-dollar bill, and told me that was the prize.

He helped me get dressed, combed my hair, and led me back to the family.

It was the first time of many torments that would last until just months before his death. His darkness led him to say just the right things to soothe and confuse a child's mind as the situation required.

At his deathbed, I forgave my Uncle Tom. At least I said the words of forgiveness. I wouldn't speak of the abuse for many, many years. Like most kids who endure abuse in their lives, I suffered it alone, quietly. I lived my childhood the best way I could: with friends, schoolmates, and family. However, the threat of Tom had always been around the next corner. When he died, it was sad for the family, but I felt free for the first time in many years. Depressed and ashamed, I kept the secret that only Uncle Tom was privy to, and had taken to his grave. He had stolen my childhood.

Chapter Eleven - The Experience of Youth

The second factor that led to my depression, and my diminished health before I entered the hospital, is a longer story. I think it builds upon the abuse inflicted by Uncle Tom. Few can survive such abuse, and then go on to a normal life without therapy. And sometimes, even therapy can't undo the damage. I was reluctant and ashamed to share what Uncle Tom had done to me. I kept hearing his words about how I was "weird." Had I shared my pain and agony with Mom or Grannie V, my path might have been much easier—perhaps I would have gotten help sooner. However, I didn't share, and I didn't get help early on. I just held the pain like a covering around me—hiding the past, hiding the horror.

Looking back at my remaining teen years, I had a great time. Oh, to be seventeen again! I had a perfect girlfriend, a strong adherence to the evangelical Methodist church, and the acceptance dedication brought. And I had many friends. Life was good.

I battled with my weight while I was a teen, and well into my twenties. However, I had moments of being close to a normal weight, and during those times, I made some great memories. I finished at the top of my class. I received a full scholarship, the Fulton Scholarship, to a nearby university. Even so, I ignored the scholarship, overlooking the opportunity for growth. Instead, I decided to take up two other pastimes after high school. One was a passion for striking fear in the hearts of others that they were going to Hell! Yes, it was a passion! It couldn't be anything less than Hell fire preaching for my beliefs at the time. I had continued to grow and be formed by the evangelical teachings of my youth. I had assimilated the belief that I had to scare as many souls as I could in order to get them into Heaven!

On the flip side, I followed a great friendship I had formed in high school with the son of a migrant farm worker and a fellow classmate named Jay. I admired him deeply, and stuck by him as a close pal. Jay represented hope, courage, faith, honesty, friendship, and understanding. I offered the same, and Hell fire preaching to boot.

After graduation from high school, I found myself working as a youth minister and scout camp counselor, and pursuing an easy Associate's degree at a little school in mid-Texas. The campus had a few buildings; holding a stake on the broad, dry plains of the land I called home. It looked as if God, Himself, had dropped a few Lego's in the middle of the Texas plains. It was not exactly what one would call a "center of higher learning," but it had the advantage of Jay's friendship. It also had the advantage of being a church outpost that would have me as a youth minister. Oh, the joy of piety!

There were a number of other colorful characters in and out of the days of my youth. One of my favorites was a girl-gone-bad whose name I won't divulge. I was out to win over her soul, and she was out to save me from boredom! Somehow our differing goals made us great friends. However, that will have to be a story for another day.

As I review my twenties, I realize they were full of instability. I bounced from my home to Dallas, where I worked for my dad, then back to west Texas to finish my degrees. I became serious about my education in my twenties, but still found plenty of room for creative bouncing! I was a psychology major, studying passionately one moment, then the next thing I knew, I was a summer youth minister being asked to quit college, and stay on full time with the church. Bounce again—back to a Texas university to explore a major in classical languages and civilizations. Then back to work for my dad in Dallas.

Now at age twenty-four, a Master of Education under my belt, I gave up my first counseling practice to work for my dad. I landed in Dallas with the lure of the promise of a great salary and, subconsciously, a chance for my father's acceptance. Bounce.

I was going to work for the man many saw as King Bob but to me was Daddy. I was a prince, who had been summoned to court. A court owned and controlled by my father. Years later, I would discover this was a place of acceptance and love. But, in my mind at the time, I was simply trying to make Dad happy.

I found myself active in the life of self exploration and self development. Seeking through many different faiths, beliefs, books, seminars, and other outlets. Driven by a need for acceptance and love. And, the need for trust and some "truth" that would explain why I had had to go through the challenges of my life up to this point.

The one growing trend throughout my twenties was my waistline! The more I felt the sting of rejection, the more I ate. I was soon weighing in at 350 pounds, and I even thought my dad avoided public appearances with me! My friends were shunning me as well. However, because I had money in my pocket, I always had fans!

Dad's company grew, and became a well known name in the automotive industry. My father reached multimillionaire status for the first time in his life, and he was generous to a fault with his employees. I was happily among them, but I had no idea of what I was going to do next. Life went on apace, the company grew larger, and so did my waistline!

In 2001, I weighed in at 414 pounds, and I was worried about my health. I had tried every diet, every miracle pill, and every hypnotherapist in Dallas. I had started and stopped diets faster than Cher changes costumes! Like most people trying these methods, I was failing miserably. I would lose twenty pounds, and gain back twenty-five! I tried Optifast when it was all the rage with Oprah, and lost seventy pounds. I gained back those seventy pounds, plus fifteen more!

I know now I was fighting the battles of self-acceptance. I was desperately unhappy with who I was, what I had been through, and the flawed perceptions I had of how my family and friends saw me. It was a feeling of painful emptiness and longing. Longing for the love and acceptance of the Creator. But, I had yet to meet Him in a way that would change my life. So, rather than seeking my spiritual side, I decided to attack my body, trying to find happiness by looking better physically. After all, you can never be too rich or too pretty! It's sad that I believed that once in my life. Not as sad, though, as the millions who continue to cling to the idea that physical perfection is all-important in the scheme of things.

Chapter Twelve – The Surgery

Even my brother and mother knew my weight was becoming a serious issue, and when the idea of bariatric surgery came up, I began to consider the option. I researched countless articles looking for the right surgery. I finally found the one that had the fewest relapses, and weight loss was guaranteed. I finally settled on a procedure called a "biliopancreatic division with a duodenal switch." The surgery would totally change the way my body absorbed food. It would rearrange my intestines to work only part of the way while food was present.

We scrutinized the surgery, and decided it was the right choice. The big problem was, the only person doing the surgery was in New York City. Dad elected to pay for the procedure out of compassion for me. He and I made several visits to New York to complete the orientation for the surgery. Every step of pre-op had to be reviewed to make certain I remained an ideal candidate for the surgery.

The BPD/DS did indeed seem the best option. It allowed for an almost miraculous amount of weight loss in a very short amount of time, with the advantage of having less than a 5% chance of regaining more than 20% of the lost weight after three years. I learned that only a handful of real people composed these statements, but the information did not make that clear. What it did make clear was a "virtual" bright red sign that said, "Fatties! Listen-up!" So, listen I did.

The surgery was to be preformed "lap," which meant it was going to be done with a large wand instrument being inserted into and out of tiny slits through my abdominal wall. I was going to become a giant fondue pot! However, rather than simply dipping and removing, they would also be slicing and dicing. And reconnecting. I never stopped to think about how terribly intricate the process was going to be.

The outline of the surgery timeline was fairly straightforward. After three hours, they were supposed to convert to an open procedure, so they could more easily lift up the stomach bulge with a snowplow! It was a theoretically safe procedure—the advantages far outweighing the risks.

They shared the risks with me. For example: I could suffer a heart attack during the procedure, or I could have a stroke, and be left paralyzed. I might also get an infection which could spread like wildfire through my intestines since almost every one of them were going to be exposed during the surgery. Not minor worries to be sure! I stopped to think for a brief moment, and then signed to give my permission for the procedure. I knew when I signed the paper that I had misgivings—no, I thought I was out of my mind!

Oh, how I wished I had listened to that inner voice. Five hours later, they wheeled me back into the surgery room. As they hefted me onto the operating table, and strapped me down, I felt a rush of dread come over me. There was a prick in the arm, a voice telling me to count backwards from 100. 99. 98. 97. Gray. So, sleepy. Black.

I regained consciousness in the operating room almost eleven hours after the surgery began. I found out later, that the procedure had taken at least six hours longer than planned. I learned later that my surgeon was instructing a fellow physician from Australia on the procedure. I would also learn the surgery was difficult, but all objectives were accomplished.

Chapter Thirteen – The Disability

As I began to regain consciousness, it felt as though my feet were on fire! I had just had my insides tossed about like a Caesar salad, and my stomach felt relatively fine. My feet, however, were in such pain that I was afraid to look at them. My mind quickly reviewed an edition of "Real Live Mistakes in Surgery" where they once took off a man's leg instead of performing the appendectomy for which he had been scheduled!

I lifted up my gown, viewing one leg and then the other. One. Two. Good! My feet continued to burn as I struggled more and more toward full consciousness. In the next moment, I was being rushed down the hall toward my ICU room. The orderly was in a great hurry, and it felt like the hospital bed was going about 75 mph, as we zoomed past the family waiting area. "Reecer!" my sister-in-law's voice shouted, and soon the family was following behind my bed at a fast clip, and in numbers that turned that hospital's surgery wing into a mini marathon! As we raced along the hall, the pain in my abdomen finally hit. It felt as if my insides were trying to come out of the little holes they'd created in my stomach!

I remember my abdomen being quite extended; it resembled a large water balloon. What a sight it must have been for the average passer-by: a very large, moaning man being raced down a hallway by an overworked orderly, and chased by a gaggle of concerned family members all trying to ask questions at once! God forgive me, but I felt like Moby Dick being chased by a Japanese whaling fleet! Or one of those overweight stars being pursued by the paparazzi on the way to Baskin-Robbins! Either way, the image was so funny in my mind that I let out a little chuckle, and was quickly delivered a corrective wince of pain from my belly.

As the staff settled me into my room where I would stay for three days of observation, they dosed medication to make me more comfortable. During that time, gases released from my stomach! There was no room for humility during that hospital stay. My whole family was there offering strong words of support. The cacophony of well-wishing faded into my head as the blessed morphine began to quiet the pain. My head swam as I hugged my father and my mother, my brother and his wife. I was going to take a nap regardless of the attention being offered. And as I drifted off in the room, fresh from surgery, clean, bandaged, and properly medicated, a bad thought continued to gnaw at my mind. Why did my feet hurt so darn much?

Chapter Fourteen – The Acceptance of Chronic Pain

As I recovered in that New York Hospital, my surgical wounds healed quickly. I began to meet all the benchmarks of complete recovery from having my insides on a low blender setting for hours. The tubes came out one by one, and the second day after the surgery, I was sitting-up on the side of the bed, not experiencing too much pain in my abdomen.

My feet were a different story. They had gone from burning, as if on fire, to feeling as if they had an ice pick stuck through them—and the pick was being pulled back and forth by some tormenting force! I had nightmares from the pain! Even in my dreams I could not escape it. A great black bird was hiding under my bed, and would slide out at night in my dreams to pick at my feet with its huge, yellow beak. I would swim back to consciousness under the delay of the morphine, until I swear I could see a flutter of black wings!

Pain, truly is a monster—a demon.

The doctors were uncertain and nervous. The head of Neurology visited, and reassured us it was a temporary condition related to the extended length of the surgery. The head surgeon visited and dismissed it again as a temporary situation. This was the best assurance the hospital board could muster. Upon leaving the hospital, my abdomen was healing well. It had endured phenomenal tampering, and now was resealing itself to its new anatomy just fine. But, man did my feet hurt!

Eventually, a year and a half later, I would be tested for nerve damage by a neurologist in Dallas. One of the best. Dad used his "power of the Rolex," and had obtained one of the best doctors available.

I was to have an ECT to look at nerve conduction damage. My brother accompanied me for this blessed event. Along the way in life, I've learned something about medical procedures, and I'm always one to offer my opinion. In addition to avoiding anything called an anal catheter, I strongly advise anyone going under an ECT to prepare for a very unhappy experience.

The doctor came in and explained he was going to test how signals traveled up and down the nerve paths from my feet to the nerve head at the base of the spine. Nerve cell pathways extend all the way down the spine, down the legs, and into the feet. The theory of the ECT is to test the health of the cell body of the nerve by applying a shock at the distal part of the nerve, and then measuring how quickly it travels to the head of the nerve. This is accomplished in the following way. First, the good doctor places a "receiver" near the groin area. Refer to the hospital note, "Thou shalt be naked." This part is a bit embarrassing, but not particularly uncomfortable. However, it's just a prelude of the fun to come!

The doctor then must insert the probe to allow the electricity to test the nerve's conduction. I knew I was in trouble when my brother's face drained of color. At first, I did not comprehend what was about to happen; I only heard the doctor say, "You'll feel a stab, and some pressure." The doctor then proceeded to stick in the gearshift lever from a 1957 Chrysler three inches into my leg! He then said, "And now I will send the current through the probe." Suddenly, the gearshift went electric, and my leg bounced around on its own! The doctor continued to grind the "gearshift" probe from drive to reverse, and back to drive. The electricity was flowing, and I felt sure my ear must be blinking out some special code language! The doctor cut the electrical current, and my leg fell back into position on the bed. The doctor frowned, and said he'd be right back. He took the gearshift with him. Thank goodness!

When he returned, there was a grave look of concern on his face. He delivered the news that the nerve cell sheath was demyelinating. That is the myelin sheath that covers the nerve cells had died, leaving the nerve body exposed to the raw electrical signals coming from the feet. Generally, these signals are muted, and correctly conveyed to the brain, they indicate touch, tickle, tap, and other signals. Mine, however, were now reporting the impact of being pierced, charred, and pummeled. The signals were not being reported accurately. Instead a fully open flow of signals was being conducted to my brain. The very simple signal sent from my toes, indicating "space and place" on the end of my feet, was being reported as fire being held to my toes! The brain couldn't do anything, but respond to the signals it received. The problem was in the "wiring." Without the necessary transformers, the circuit was thrown wide open, and the result was constant fiery pain.

We asked the doctor to run the test again in a month to see if there had been any change, but he refused. Flatly. "These conditions do not heal," he explained. It was a defective nerve now, and it would be defective for the rest of my life.

For the first year or two, it didn't really sink in that I would have chronic pain for life. The pain was controlled by more and more aggressive opiate therapy. In year four, the pain became too much for oral pain medications. My body's natural tolerance had been kicked-in, and I turned to surgical interventions as depression took hold. A spinal cord stimulator (SCS) was placed, but failed to be effective because the leads migrated. A replacement was introduced, however, it had to be removed when a staph infection was evident.

In years five and six of my chronic pain experience, I met my current pain specialist who also placed and removed two

SCS devices into my body. Finally, he placed a morphine pump with the lead going directly into my spine. Relief was sweet, but short-lived. Again, my body exerted its tolerance, and soon the pump was delivering stronger levels of medication. The "normal" pain level for my life went from a level three to a level four, on a one-to-ten pain scale. Then to a level five! To compare this pain to something imaginable, it was about the same pain as being punched in the face hard enough to loosen teeth. Now, as I write this, my "normal" pain level is a five or six. What the future holds on this front is unknown. However, as I count back twenty different physicians, eighteen different surgical interventions, acupuncture, meditation, visualization, and various other treatments, one thing is sure, it wasn't boring! "But, God, the feet still hurt. Thank you, God that they don't hurt more!"

Chapter Fifteen – Surviving the Demon

Chronic pain sounds ominous. However, the experience of it can be darker than any gathering storm. The prospect offered-up to me was simply that I live with relatively no changes in my body's ability to function save one caveat: each second will be excruciatingly painful! This is the chronic pain of "cryptogenic sensory poly-neuropathy." It was the final diagnosis for my condition. Life, then, was lived in a court of law, the United States Federal Court for the Northern District of the State of New York. I plead my case against my surgeon. It was decided that something did, indeed, happen to my nerves during the BPD/DS surgery. However, what it was that caused the nerves to die, to begin to shed open their delicate coverings and convert them to dead flesh, was unknown. It could have been the pressure to the spine caused by the misstep of an anesthesia team. It could have been the slip of the surgeon's knife. It could have been the padding on the operating table. The Court decided no one had meant for it to happen, and no one could have prevented it from happening. However, it had happened. No monies or damages would be awarded. No action against the surgeon or the team would be taken. So, for the rest of my life, it will be the nature of some of my nerves to be connected to their dead counterparts. That is, until healing comes.

I wake each day, the sheath covering my nerves leading to each of my feet, dead and open. My good nerves report their horror at being connected to their dead brethren through electrical signals up the nerve endings. The corresponding response is pain—burning, stabbing pain, every second of every day. Others suffer the same pain and worse. Those who are going through the end stages of cancer, ALS, or other diseases, suffer greatly. Those who are aging, and find their bodies failing them, experience the pain of general neuropathy.

It was a hard adjustment, and it took me through some very dark places. The first years were the hardest while going from physician to physician seeking help. I picked up many labels from "drug-seeker" to an outright "liar." If the nerve conduction study had not confirmed the nerve damage, if I had not happened upon the intelligent, successful physicians who care for me today, I would have been lost on the way—lost to drugs the way some are who deal with chronic pain.

In the first years, though, I had neither the right diagnosis, nor the right intervention. I had only the pain, and very limited skills at managing the ever-present nemesis. I could not find help legally, so I did what many do, I sought to medicate the pain. I sought physical relief through alcohol, and vices. I sought relief through troubled relationships with troubled souls. I felt as if I must have done something to have deserved the pain. I felt bad. I felt guilty. And, eventually, I felt depressed.

Depression is an insidious foe because it does not announce itself immediately. It comes on slowly at first. You begin to lose joy in the things which once brought you great happiness. People who love you are driven away as you isolate yourself because you think of yourself as a bad person. Unclean. The depression came hidden within the pain. As my body began to tolerate medications and require larger and larger doses of narcotics to control the pain, the depression flourished. I found myself longing to be rid of this life. Nothing was fun anymore. I had no interest in friends, much less relationships. Then, my encompassing thoughts were about ending my own life. I sought suicide once with great conviction. I failed at that too. And my foolish attempt to end my life did not end the chronic pain. It was still there, like the rest of me, lingering, pressing, depressing.

Chapter Sixteen – Giving in to Depression

In the spring of 2006, I had had all I could take. I don't know what the trigger point was exactly. I think I had simply given up. I had taken to drinking alcohol as much as I could before passing out each day. Pain was my constant companion until alcoholic unconsciousness took me under for a few hours. My family watched in horror, helpless to stop me—helpless to stop the hurting. I deflected their efforts at every turn, leaving them frustrated and angry at times. I did not want help. I wanted off the planet! I had no awareness of a loving Creator. I had no desire to talk to the God who had cursed me with this unwanted pain companion.

I began to hate myself. I began to hate myself so badly that I avoided mirrors. I avoided washing my clothes. I avoided eating regular meals. I did every mean and cruel thing to myself you can imagine.

Finally, I decided it must all end. Depression had become despair, and I set my mind on suicide. I planned to drive my car off an embankment near Austin, Texas. The car seemed to drive itself as the speed reached 100 miles per hour. I reached the embankment and – kaboom. I remember I was briefly airborne. Then nothing but blackness as I soared into the abyss. There is nothing glorious about it. There is nothing romantic about it. It was an evil and desperate reaction to a life situation I did not think I could bear. It was wrong. I was wrong.

The attempt to derail myself did not work. It did land me in trouble with the courts, and with my family on its last leg. I cannot recall the months that followed, but I know that I spent time away from reality. When my body was sober, the pain was unbearable, and I continued the cycle of medicating with alcohol to pass out. I write these words as an acknowledgement to others who are suffering chronic pain. Please find help! Please do not close doors. Please do not give up. There are many opportunities to hate yourself, and hurt yourself. The demon of pain will offer the forbidden to provide a temporary escape, but the result could be the loss of your identity. Like drunk, junkie, psychotic "friends"—they wait for you to give in. Do not go down that path. I did. I have seen things of evil no one should ever see, and have experienced the darkest nights. It led me to the doorstep of death. It opened me to horrible disease and infection. It led me to a hospital in north Dallas—weak with septic organs, and primed for the first disease that would take me for the ride of my life.

If you love those who are hurting, believe them passionately! Help them find good physicians. Give them time to grieve their loss of the life they knew before chronic pain. Help them find good resources in physicians and therapists. Accommodate them into your lives in their limited ability to participate. When they make reasonable requests, grant them. However, when they push boundaries, stand firm, and help them with a reality check. Most of all, when they apologize, forgive them, and embrace them as if they have done no wrong. "Dad, Ross, Mom, I'm sorry about those times."

Now back to my path…

Chapter Seventeen – Before the Miracle

My memories of that first hospital that admitted me, are few and far between. I had pneumonia, and I couldn't get enough oxygen into my body to keep things functional at anything approaching normal. But I have a few memories about my stay that I can recount. It was there that I learned the basics—a boot camp if you will for future hospital stays. One of the first rules I learned: someone else was in control of my life. Second, nude and semi-nude seemed to be a fact of life. Third, I learned humility quickly when dignity found no place. From time to time, I was given a menu, but the final options were up to the nutritionists.

The eggs described as "fluffy and light, sure to put a smile on the start of your day," arrived rubbery like that Chinese fake puke. Toast, which was described to have been "made from our bakery fresh daily," had the texture of the finest shingles available from a local rooftop! Jokes are common about hospital food, so I won't go through them all. I do now, though, subscribe to the theory there is a kernel of truth in all that humor.

Being out of control is not something anyone likes to experience. However, in the hospital, it is an "in your face" kind of controlling, and in particular regarding your diet, that gets to you! And elimination of said food is another control issue! Being out of control includes irregular toileting! The very utterance of the term "catheter" still brings horror to my mind. I had the pleasure of experiencing one called the Foley Catheter. It is for the urethra. Why on earth anyone would wish to have their perfectly good family name associated with this indignity, I have no idea! I guess there are limits. After all, there is no name for the bedpan except bedpan! It's not called a "Smith Collector," or some such thing.

I learned quickly that nothing—nothing is equal to your mom showing up at the beginning of visiting hours every morning. Even if she arrived while you are receiving a Foley Catheter! I was elated, always, to see her! I would often wake well before the 6:00 AM hour which ushered in the first visiting period to the protest of the night staff. Sometimes my morning would begin at 2:00 or 3:00 AM. Those were the lucky mornings. When you are lying on your back, in the still of the night, hopelessly attached to your bed, your IV tubes, the machine happily pinging in the corner, you have precious time to think. I remember I would play a little game of counting the dots on the ceiling tiles, and then see if I could beat my record in the next minute. Oh, what good times I had!

Then, gloriously, at the appointed time, every morning for over 150 mornings, my mother would come. A push at the door would announce her entrance. Yes, depending on "who" pushed the door, the hinge noise varied. There was the push of the timid, newly certified technicians, which provided very little squeak at all. They really were, I think, as afraid of me as I was of them. There was the push of the doctor—self-assured, authoritarian swoosh-bang, and they are in the room for a look at the chart. "Hello, Mr. Ummm...." A few flips of the paperwork, a scribble on my page, and they were gone. Then there was the push of the nurse—more at home than anyone! This was her territory, and I was simply visiting. These were her rooms, her halls, and her space. Nurses ruled and don't you forget it. However, no better sound at the door would ever come than the push that heralded the sweetest sound in the world—my name spoken from the lips of my Mom.

Names identify who we are by those who know us. It was not just the joy of hearing my own name, but the unbridled happiness of my name being called by the first person who ever loved me—my mom. The only thing that comes close is having your father show-up, and scare the staff into action. My dad stands 6'4", and is a man whose presence commands respect. It is not just his demeanor, but the large Rolex he wears, that makes medical staff unsure if he is a visitor, or perhaps an "undercover physician."

The direct care staff tried hard, but it seemed to me (at the time) that they were not among God's most compassionate beings. It was during a boom of the economy, and the only people working at the bottom of the totem positions, were people who were desperately needed for staffing quotas.

The nursing staff would buzz away for a few seconds when my mother would arrive, confused because their monotony had been broken, and because my mom carried herself with the bearing of a nurse. However, they would scatter like roaches when my father arrived! If the number one rule of being in the hospital was "Thou Shalt Not Have Power," then the second one was certainly, "Thy Mother and Thy Father are Your Only Hope!" And, hope they were. I felt their prayers.

The earlier fiasco came to an end in mid-December when they discharged me with a blood oxygen level of eighty-five. I was to be released to home healthcare with a full recovery predicted. That would not happen. Within two weeks, I was checked into what I would call "home" for the next four and a half months: a hospital in north Dallas. I had been dutifully carried there by ambulance, and quickly admitted with Pneumonia and MRSA. This was a deadly combination the doctor would later comment about, "Wow, never heard of anyone living through one of those." He was right. And he was wrong. The journey was an interesting one for the next few months.

Chapter Eighteen – When I Crossed

I arrived at the local hospital on a cold day, December 17, 2007. The only clear memory I have of the day is how frigid it was. Although I was only exposed from the ambulance door to the entryway of the Emergency Room, the cold bit through me, and I noticed the gray sky hovering above me. The sound of the ambulance doors opening, imitated hammers striking on a large spike. Two strikes. I don't know how or why I remember that detail, but the sounds are still perfectly clear. I can still remember hearing them resonate as somber harbingers of the things to come in the next few days of my life.

I spent January on a ventilator—rather on-and-off a ventilator. The days on outweighed the days off of the ventilator. My lungs were under a virulent attack, and the oxygen levels of my blood were dropping. At the same time, the abuse I had done to my liver raged its own wars on the rest of my organs. I was on the edge of the grave, and there was nothing I could do to change it.

The end of December, Christmas and its celebrations, went unremembered by me. My thirty-ninth birthday in January, again found me on a drip of Adavan and morphine, and a machine was breathing for my body. My lungs were filled with fluid, and I remember I made gurgling noises when I tried to talk during my conscious moments. It was during this time, somewhere between the intubations, midway through my battle, that I crossed over into the Light. And returned.

Waking up, crying to myself in the ICU, I was back. It was dark in the room. The gloom was palpable. I was back, and I wasn't happy about it at all. It seemed only seconds before I had been in the Source with all the love and knowledge, hope and understanding of the Creator at my side. Now, I was in a room, alone, after the team removed me from the ventilator. Never had I felt such a sense of abandonment. My being ached to remove the overwhelming monotony I felt. It seemed as though the pause between every tick of the second hand on the prominently displayed clock, spread out like a huge blanket of isolation.

In those hours, I went through the darkest emotions. I wondered what the response would be if I pulled out the IV's from my arm. I may even have tried. My body was so weak I could barely move my head, much less yank out a needle that felt the size of a log. Unable to lift my head made me even more anxious. Not only was I back from paradise; I had arrived home to a broken body. It was like having to trade in a Corvette for a Yugo—a Yugo without a steering wheel at that!

Slowly, I fought the depression monster, and won, when an hour later, hope and faith returned with a push of the door. My mom arrived in a blue coat. The textured material that made up the outer layer of her jacket, made the most wonderful rustling noise. But it wasn't a sound that made the moment, it was the sight of her!

Relief warmed my mother's face like a thousand rosy dawns. Her grin beamed me a warm "welcome back to the world of the living." I guess something must have clicked inside of me in those first few moments of the very first visit I received after returning from death. I knew in my core being that I was going to be okay. I had a purpose, and I was loved.

More joy came to me when I rolled out of ICU and back to my room at the hospital. My sister-in-law had "grown" a garden of family photos for me. Each photo was a happy slice of life. Although I could not smell, taste, hear, or feel the images as I had during the crossing over, they were, nevertheless, a happy sight for me. A whole field of faces who cared about me deeply, and were all glad I was back.

Things began to get better, at least physically, from that day forward. My father, mother, and brother visited daily. I had been quarantined from the rest of the hospital because of the MRSA. I was a plague in the land of the ill, but my brave family came to visit me each day. Being quarantined from others in the hospital did have its advantages. The best perk was having a private room. Funny, I never really understood how the virus beleaguering my system was supposed to know how to read the "Stop! Isolation Precautions in Effect!" sign on my room door but I guess it made a difference to someone in charge.

The virus working on my lungs was so dangerous, that everyone who entered my room had to don a gown and a mask in order to come in. It was an odd thing at first, seeing family members in latex gloves and sneeze protectors. It looked as though they were there to perform surgery.

The days ahead consisted of more battles, however, and I fought through each intubation without crossing again. The very last trip to the ventilator came in April. I had ordered a cheeseburger, and had somehow managed to suck part of it into my left lung! I don't recommend eating hospital beef, much less trying to breathe it. It quickly caused my lung infection to multiply. The virus, which had obviously never been to McDonalds, went after the hamburger as if it were on the dollar menu!

Chapter Nineteen – Recovering from the Miracle

May 5, 2008 dawned warm and bright in a Dallas suburb. I was taking my last wheelchair tour of the grounds of the Integrated Physical Rehabilitation Hospital. I had survived my trial by fire, and I was going home that day. While I was happy for the final curtain call on CiDif and anal catheters, I was also terribly, terribly disturbed. I was rolling out of the hospital, and into a world of pain, hurt, and confusion that only a few weeks ago, I thought I had escaped forever. Home. It was not a thought filling me with overwhelming joy, but at most, a mild dread. A cloud passed over the sun as I exited the hospital, and the coolness was immediate on my feet. My feet. They had been on fire non-stop since they had let my implanted pump go dry in the hospital for fear of it depressing my respiratory rate. Getting the pump refilled was a priority for me. At least then, the unbearable pain would be masked somewhat.

Of course, the pain in my feet had not been my priority during the last few days. My rehab and occupational therapy had been the biggest of recent challenges. I had learned that my body-self was still quite unsure about the whole concept of getting from my bed to a sitting position, much less walking with a walker down the hall. After all, I was sure the nursing staff sneaked into my room, and buttered the bottom of my walker with devious glee! What else could make the thing so hard to handle? The walker would take on a life of its own as I aimed it down the hall, and over the green and blue tiles spreading out in front of me like an ocean. I would think to myself "full forward," while the device would decide "hard to keel" was a much more amusing direction!

Regardless of the amount of amusement I had provided for the staff, insurance codes must be followed, and the limit for the amount of necessary recovery time had been met. In other words, I was out of days, and it was time to go home. Home.

There was that word again. I knew what home was supposed to be now. I had been sent back to talk about it— about our Creator, our purpose here on earth, about love, and not judging others harshly (or ourselves.) Following a homecoming like that, what could possibly measure up? There was nothing I could do but get back to work here on the planet, and see what a difference I could make in others' lives, and in my own. I had not been kind to others in ways, but mostly, I had not been kind to myself.

However, one does not cross from life to death and back again bringing with them a secret toll-free tech. support number! There is no search index for reviewing topics beginning with "I" for "Instant Fulfillment of Agreements." I would learn that in the months to come, but at the time, I was completely lost—feeling as if I were on "hold" with heaven's "customer support line" when I prayed.

I released the wheelchair as it came to the lip of the ramp on the sidewalk. It was a simple little thrill that I had learned to relish daily. Getting the chair to the top of the slope made my arms burn, and my heart would beat faster as I gained altitude. I would close my eyes and pretend I was mountain climbing, or boarding a scuba diving boat. Whoosh! I would go down over the lip to find a moment of complete floating joy. Momentarily, I existed without gravity, and was accelerating just as my "true form" had done in the crossing. The ride always ended too soon. And it usually made me very, very sad.

Today, though, was different. As I opened my eyes, my mother seemed to appear out of nowhere. Her smile was that of a mother surveying her newborn. I never fail to be humbled by it. God smiles upon us every day of our lives the same way—with the smile of a parent observing His children. That parental smile, taken to infinite power, is how God loves us. Here on Earth, you can glimpse a God-smile by visiting a hospital's nursery window. Now there's a Norman Rockwell moment! And in spite of our family's humanness, we experienced those surreal Rockwell moments too.

Alongside Mom was Roxie. She was radiant because she'd just been to the spa. She literally jumped into my lap. As her tongue busily explored my face and ears, she pushed her body against mine, seeking, and giving support to her "daddy." She wriggled with glee, and proceeded to literally engulf me with kisses and nuzzles. No, she was not a lover. She was better—she was a fat, fine, fifty pound English bulldog, and she had just discovered that her pack leader was alive and well!

She excitedly launched herself from me, to my mom, and back again. Oh, she was gloriously happy! In that moment, something deep inside my spirit-self stirred. With one of those licks, tears started flowing that would not end for many minutes. I don't think a single one escaped the tongue of Roxie, and I soon found myself in the suds of doggy drool! What unconditional love!

I may not have been knocking on heaven's door at that moment, but I had delivered "heaven" to Roxie with my presence. It was a good day with love surrounding me.

The following day, and days thereafter, the weather was gloomy, making my mood much the same. They say it gets worse before it gets better, and it is a truth that can't be denied. I closed my spirit-self off from everybody and everything that might have helped me heal. Despite my crossing over, I had much to learn here on the earth plane. I have very little memory of the events that happened the first month after leaving the hospital, and before arriving at Oakdale* Mental Health System's Trauma Program.

* Note: Oakdale is a fictitious name which has been used to protect the innocent.

Chapter Twenty – Getting Beyond "Crazy"

During my five and half month battle against MRSA pneumonia, and the host of opportunistic infections and ailments accompanying it, life had continued to move forward. So had my connections to it. I was left to recount the experience of the crossing again and again in my mind while everyone else in my life was trying to bring me back up to speed.

Memories of those days move across a fuzzy, dispassionate screen in my mind. Memories of a trip to the county court to plead guilty to a two year old suicide attempt in which I had totaled a beautiful red convertible. As the judge sized me up, she seemed to decide I was worthy of her sympathy, and I was placed on six-month probation for operating a motor vehicle while under the influence of medication. Which, how much, and what kind of medication, whether self-prescribed or legitimate, was left to the county clerk to fill in. It ranked a memory because it caused me to visit the same streets which, ten years before, took me to classes for my Masters of Education degree in professional counseling.

I wondered if my professors would have looked on me with shame, or simple intellectual curiosity. I hoped the latter. I did not want to bring shame to the program that had once made me a great helping professional. I also wondered if they felt I had taken the classes as an attempt at self-therapy? I was well aware that some do.

I wish I had heeded the first words written on the chalkboard by my very first professor, Dr. Garcia, at Texas State. He wrote, simply: "Get a therapist." It was the greatest wisdom I would take from that school.

The same state that had declared me a Master, now had declared me a misdemeanant. I remember riding back from the courthouse to Dallas with my father. I felt shame; like a small child whose father had just finished scolding him. We exchanged perhaps two words. By now, I was regaining a bit of strength, and with the strength had come more awareness of how badly it still hurt to move. Or, even worse, sit still.

There are still the terrible memories of the dreams that haunted me in that time between the hospital stay and my time in the mental health center. The great black bird, pain that pecked my feet during sleep seemed to come nightly. As my wounds and sores healed, the old, chronic pain made itself ever more known to me. In my dreams, the bird would tear at my toes, and in my waking, slowed by the medication; I would find it sitting on the end of my bed as I came to consciousness.

Dreams of the Crossing gave me temporary respite. That place of such pure, perfect happiness would come to my sleeping visions with the promises of its existence. For a split second, I would remember the painless freedom as if it were going to be there when I awoke. Instead I would feel myself fall, all knowledge passing out of my mind as I came close to waking. And in waking, I would experience the feet pulsing in pain—my brain void of the things it once treated as child's play, and my spirit-self all but lost to me. The dreams bothered me, so I began sleeping less and less.

My body was weak. It had been through so much in the hospital. I dangled between life and death for many, many days during my stay. The time on the ventilator seemed to drain my body's energy as if I had gone five rounds with Mike Tyson. The cumulative effect had also dropped my weight to where I was skin and bones. I remember looking at myself in the mirror, and thinking how ironic it was that my reflection had once filled the mirror from end to end, and now I looked like a badly pitched, flapping tent.

I had shrunk while I was in the hospital. The doctors still hadn't been able to figure out exactly what happened. However, my stature had gone from 5'11" to 5'9". I had been a bit taller than my mother, but now she was taller than me. It was just two inches, but it seemed to make a world of difference to the part of my mind-self that had equated height with greatness.

Finally, at some point in this insanity, I was led to the breaking point where my behavior so disturbed my mother that she turned to an outside source to find help for me. I had become moody, angry, and inconsolable in my pain. I had begun to break from reality and lapse into a madness that was ugly and raging. In this wasteland, blowing wild and seething with hate for life, the Creator reached out His hand and shaped my mother's thoughts to find help for me. Mom packed my bags, drove me up to the Oakdale entrance, and left me as I madly shouted out how I wanted white roses on my coffin. No good bye, no I love you, just desperation on her part to help. There was also desperation within my spirit-self for recognition from my mind-self. My mind-self was so blinded by pain, confusion, and loss that it had all but given up, though my spirit-self kept tugging just the same.

I was evaluated by the intake team, and in their wisdom and kindness, I landed in the Trauma Unit based on the work of Dr. Z. Here, the healing would begin.

Chapter Twenty One - The Journey Back

Oakdale

There is really no easy way to come to grips with the fact one is in an inpatient mental health facility. There is the fact that you are in a place where you cannot leave at will, you cannot eat in the middle of the night, you cannot go outside to have a walk at will. On the long-list, most of my questions were answered with a simple, "No."

I was in the land of No. I was one of twenty in the "No unit!" Here, being "in the No" meant admitting you had no clue. I fit the profile readily as I entered the group. I was clueless how to handle the things in my life, which were spiraling out of control like a persistent vortex. I had only resolved myself to the fact that I was going to be on the planet until I had completed my path. I did not have to like it. No, I did not like it at all!

Oakdale was a beautiful mental health care facility. It had sprawling grounds that offered restful lawns. When they weren't saying, "No," I could walk the short paths between the buildings. I knew that others had been there and found peace too. I could trace the outlines of where the old swimming pool had been, and sense the laughter of earlier residents. I could walk through the old white house where the first residents and their physicians had lived fulltime, and know that healing of some sort or another had taken place.

Then there is the other side of things. "Patient evaluation and intake," sounds like a fairly straightforward process. For the patient, it is more akin to a police booking. This was after all, a hospital, and I knew the drill for the hospital. "Thou Shalt Have No Power" is the mantra no matter how much you dress it up in bad faux pearls and cubic zirconium. Such was the presence of my "Intake Coordinator." She was a short, curtly lady with the demeanor of a Gulag officer! Then came the intake interview! Now we were getting somewhere.

"Reece," began Dr. Y., "How can we help you today?" I don't remember the exact conversation that followed. I do remember that Dr. Y. had strategically positioned himself between the door and me, either to prevent my escape, or to facilitate his own exit should I become "difficult." The room was pleasant, but devoid of any decorative "heavy" objects. Dr. Y was no fool. I answered the question, and it was sufficient enough for Dr. Y. to sit down, bend forward, and dutifully take interest in my words. I remember it because it seemed a genuinely kind gesture. In such institutions, duty was the order of the day, and genuine kindness was something rather rare. His voice had been calm and soothing as I tried to convince him mightily that I was not crazy, but I didn't know how to live a life full of pain, confusion, and need when there was a perfect paradise just a "death" away. Apparently, telling a psychiatrist that you have been to the "other side," and have returned with wisdom and kindness to share with the world, does not get you a sane certificate! Instead, you are "processed" to an Intake Coordinator. So there I sat with Miss K. trying to focus my sight, bathing her big plastic pearls with my tears.

"Mr. Manley, you have been admitted to the Trauma Unit here at Oakdale," she said in an ominous tone. "We will have to get the paperwork together. You will sit here, and I will be back. Please do not leave the room. Please give me your wallet. Please give me the contents of your pockets. Please give me your shoelaces." "Please stand on your head and babble happily until I return!" Those could have been her last words as she gathered up everything, and continued to command the essentials of the process. I was collapsing inside, and the best they could do was to take my shoelaces?

Miss K. struck me as funny as she gathered up all of my identification, insurance cards, and wallet contents. Her eyes lit up when she saw I had supplemental insurance, and then down just as quickly when she saw the Medicare card. I had evidently caused another ream of paperwork by carrying the little red, white, and blue card. I had observed the same look on the face of my bulldog when I had accidentally mentioned her favorite treat out loud, and then failed to deliver. Miss K. left me to muddle over life for a few moments while she began the shuffle of documentation that would relinquish my will to the powers-that-be of the hospital. When she returned, she had a thick packet and a camera. The smell of the cigarette she had grabbed, while she had been waiting on administrative staff to spit out paperwork on patient number 808172, lingered on her clothing like a sad gray ghost. Yet, there was something reassuring about the fact that she had taken the time to return to her routine life of grabbing a smoke while I felt mine was falling apart! Miss K. apparently thought life was going to go right on, regardless of what happened to 808172. Perhaps I could think she was right long enough to get through the process. The process took me right along indeed. The tour of the Trauma Unit began. Ticket number 808172 now moving along the corridor.

As we left the white house, we walked the short sidewalk between the older structure and the new campus where the Lewis Unit was located. The Lewis Unit would be my home for three weeks. The building opened into two long halls beyond the front doors. We stepped onto the elevator and arrived at the second floor. A welcoming sign reading "Warning: This is a locked unit!" greeted me as we walked from the elevator. Now arriving: Mr. 808172. Room for one.

Chapter Twenty Two – Trauma Unit

There was a big living room area, called the common room, group room, or meeting room depending on who was directing said meeting. Patients were two to a room with one private bathroom inside the room. There were twenty of us: two males and eighteen females. I would soon learn this was not an accurate count though, after you included the (Dissociative Identity Disorder) DID-diagnosed patients. Bringing in the alter personalities to the headcount, we were about forty total. I guess the ratio isn't to exceed two to a body on the unit at any given time. Good thing, too, since naming the alter identity was a game much enjoyed on the unit!

The common room opened-up into a dining area at the far end; this was also locked. The only other room was the "Sanctuary," the patient's name for the smoking room. The door would make a great whooshing sound, as if you were visiting the Mighty Oz! The room was a ten-by-ten square, nicotine-stained cubicle. The whooshing sound came from the air scrubbers installed to contain the nicotine and noxious fumes from others on the unit who didn't smoke. Six people were non-smokers, if you remember to count the alter personalities in the equation!

In all of my years of experimenting with substances, tobacco is not one I had tried. I would learn quickly that the only way to be accepted in the group was to join others in the cigarette-sanctuary away from staff's prying eyes and ears. Those with paranoia disorders would say the room was bugged. But, that was okay; they had their aluminum foil hats to keep them safe. Darn government spies. Alien spies. Russian spies. Of course, it depended on the time of day as to when the spies would be listening in.

Programming and routine is part of the therapeutic milieu of any mental health center. Part of getting better is acting like you're better. If you want to function in society, you've got to take some baby steps. From "how to make my bed" to "yes, I always flush the toilet," I had the basics introduced. Amazingly enough, I got it down pretty much the first day. A gold sticker went up somewhere to mark my progress. I was proud of myself; I knew to place my sheets into the blue (not the white) laundry cart!

I acclimated. I wrote in my journal. I attended groups. I dutifully carried on housekeeping. But mostly I gave myself permission to listen.

I remember the fourth night. I was lying in bed, feet still aflame with the angry power of damaged nerves, present even in this place, hidden away from humanity's view. I cried and reached out with everything I had for God. And, that night, God came.

Chapter Twenty Three – God in the Room

The room was quiet save the snoring of the six foot, four inch, 210 pound roommate of mine who suffered from DID. This gentle giant of a person would sometimes slip into a frightened mind-self of a five-year-old child. However, on this night, he was slumbering in the loud, intentional way a twenty-six-year-old body does, having taken a large dose of Seroquel.

As I cried and asked God silently, "Why, why, why?" over and over again in my mind, my roommate stirred in his bed. I heard him rise to his feet and plod to the center of the shared room. I saw him stand there as if suspended between wake and sleep. I was just about to get up and help him back to bed, when he spoke.

The voice was kind. He usually either sounded very much like a child, demure and slightly embarrassed, or like a big, old redneck Texan giving away his oilfield background. But tonight, he came across as simply warm as he spoke.

"Reece," he began. "You know you are loved. Now just chill out, and quit asking why, and ask why not! Quit asking when, and ask how to spend your time. Quit asking why me, and start saying thank you for who I am. Guess that's about it!" he concluded. He turned and asked the air for permission to go back to bed. The air acquiesced. He returned to bed, and was asleep in a few moments. It was the first important part of the listening I would do. It was the beginning of listening that would allow me to see my crossing to the Light as a miracle, not as a missed chance for heaven. And so I listened. The insanity of running thoughts, images, questions, and memories began to settle, beginning the following morning.

Each day started with a community group. All members of the unit gathered in the day room, the official term for the large, open area with four rows of chairs and benches facing each other in a square formation. We would report on three things. We reported our physical feelings, our emotional state, and our goal for the day. One, two, three. That was what it took, for the therapists working with us, to know how to begin their sessions with us for the day. It was also an alert for us to watch out for other patients who were having a bad day.

I am struck by the ability of the group process to bring out honesty. There is something wonderful, and terrible that happens when twenty people are gathered together, knowing they've been to the ends of their respective ropes. If someone says they are having a bad day, it means they are having a BAD day—especially on the Trauma Unit.

Bad days often consisted of reliving memories, and the sharing of those memories comes fast. It was hoped that by sharing, we would draw strength by spreading the horror of being isolated—held prisoner by one mind. In sharing it with the group, we could find support, strength, and absolution. From the woman who readily, unemotionally recounted her father burning her with cigarettes, to the veteran recalling the disappearing of his best friend's head in a vapor of blood and dust, the Trauma Unit was not for the weak! It was for those of us who had had life-altering experiences that were beyond our control. But the events had happened, and someone had to own it, review it, assimilate it, and live with it. The "it" being a different thing for each one of us there. Yes, there were similar themes, but each one had its own unique horror. The good thing about horror is that it ends. But while you are enduring it, it can be a savage visitor to the soul!

That morning, I reported: "Physically, I am in pain. Emotionally, I'm," Oh, heck! I had planned to say my usually reported statement 'hopeful God will change my life'. It would not come out, finally, after three false starts, I got it said, "…confident that change is taking place today." The group didn't seem to note the change between hope and confidence, but the spark had taken place in my own thinking, and I approached the process differently.

This program, this three-week break from the duties of reality, was my God-granted time to take what had happened to me, explore it and let it change me and my outlook. It was not to be a three week lesson in wallowing in self pity. I am ashamed to admit that was how I had originally approached it. However, in shifting from hope to confidence, this plan was going to be transforming. I had set in motion a series of events that would take me, not only from the dark, lost place I was in, to a place of leveled feelings and acceptance, but beyond the zero sum balance to discover life in the positive numbers region.

Chapter Twenty Four – Meeting the Chief

One of the most powerful therapists on the Unit, powerful in effectiveness and in rank, was Dr. Z. He was the architect of the Trauma Unit, and a disciple of the cognitive theories of counseling. Cognitive theories rely on the mind-self to be the seat of change, and of current theories, it offers the most hope for not only feeling better, but for achieving a happier, more productive life. Dr. Z. had spent a great deal of time considering the effects of traumatic events on patients' ability to provide rational reactions to current stimulus.

When Dr. Z. works with a patient, it is done in a group setting. Sessions with him are considered "gold" by patients with intentions of getting better. There was a waiting list for appointments with Dr. Z., and I placed my name on that list. I waited anxiously for the day when I would have the opportunity to work with him.

In the meantime, there were a number of days when just the day-to-day events of the unit were God's teaching tools. Some of them were humorous. Some of them were terribly sad, but all were life lessons.

Chapter Twenty Five – "CPR! CPR!"

I mentioned DID earlier. This is the new diagnostic term for MPD or multiple personality disorders. Many people scoff at the idea of the condition existing at all, however, Oakdale is one of the nation's imminent treatment centers, and we attracted the real thing. One patient, we'll call her Ann, had at least three identified personalities. Each would interact with the public independently of the other. The split in Ann's personality had happened when she was a girl, exposed to ritual abuse too horrible for her young mind to handle. In its defense, it had created another safe place to go. Another personality in which to hide during the most horrible of crimes against her. In her adult life, the personalities had continued. So powerful was the change, Ann's alter personalities would actually require different things from her body-self. For example, she needed glasses when she was in one alter state, and then had 20/20 vision when she was herself (Ann.)

Of course, DID is very difficult to diagnose, and very easy to fake on the part of a patient simply seeking the attention. One such attention seeker was Lisa. Lisa was a buxom and beautiful young twenty-something lady who said she had an alter personality responsible for her drug use, and her lifestyle as a stripper. Lisa called this part of herself, Sherry. While Lisa was rational and respectful, Sherry was seductive, impulsive, and had a habit of taking off her shirt. When a personality shift occurs, it usually occurs in the face of a "trigger." A trigger is some type of outside stimuli which startles or reminds the DID patient of the original event which triggered the personality change. Triggers can be violent actions, loud noises, angry yelling. Or, it can be subtler such as a smell or hearing a familiar song.

On day eleven in the Trauma Unit, we had a triggering event. The day was normal through breakfast. Everyone had attended, eaten the morning meal, taken hygiene breaks, and then gathered for morning group. And, of course, we visited the Sanctuary of Nicotine.

I was in the smoking sanctuary when it happened. The sound was loud and piercing. It was several decibels louder than any other alarm I had heard, and it made me jump. It was the fire alarm on the unit, and it was peeling through the pre-lunch life of the unit with an immediate, insistent urgency.

Along the hallways, emergency lighting popped on, and fire doors automatically unlocked as the alarm wailed.

The staff was out among us in seconds, ushering patients to line up against the wall for evacuation from the unit should it be more than just a drill. Much excitement was to follow. It seems the sound had triggered the alter personality of Sherry out of the patient, Lisa. Sherry (Lisa) emerged from her room topless and ready to go onstage. She approached one new patient and demanded to be escorted to her stage so she could dance. The new patient was discombobulated by the events to the point that her response was simply to scream. Sherry was not expecting a scream. She ran to a staff member on the other side of the unit, and demanded to know what was going on.

That staff member knew Sherry, and tried her best to take her hand while explaining she needed to find a shirt because she might have to exit the building. Of the long, calm explanation, Sherry heard only the word, fire!

"Fire! Fire!" screamed Sherry, bounding from room-to-room. A staff member who had grabbed a tee shirt, and was shouting at Sherry to put on the shirt, pursued her. Sherry did not seem to take any notice of the staff member, and continued to bellow, and flap, and bellow, as her body's attributes shared airspace with almost every square inch of the unit.

Sherry stopped suddenly, and the pursuing staff member crashed into her. "Wait, what do we do in a fire?" Sherry asked loudly (of no one but herself!) "We do CPR, CPR, CPR!" Sherry cried out, and within a second, Sherry was upon us insisting we all needed CPR because there was a fire! However, Sherry's idea of CPR required reciprocal action. "I'll CPR you, if you CPR me!" she offered to each resident. At this point, the staff had managed to get most of us against the evacuation wall. The alarm continued to scream. One of the patients was shouting that the sprinklers would soon be on, and would be showering us with hydrochloric acid! Sherry finally reached the other male on the unit, who earnestly agreed to her request. It was love at first CPR! The staff moved to separate the two, and clothe Sherry. The rest of us completely lost it at the silliness of the scene. It was what the staff would refer to as a BAD day. However, as far as I know, the term "I CPR You," survives as an inside joke on the Trauma Unit of Oakdale to this day!

Chapter Twenty Six – When Hope Failed

And then there were dark moments on the unit—times when hope could not be rallied despite the best efforts of staff, therapists, psychiatrists, and even patients. One man had come to the Unit after a break up with his fiancé. Jacob, I will call him, had a long history of being abandoned in his early childhood. When he found his fiancé was having an affair, Jacob fell into a deep depressive state. As he found his way to the Trauma Program at Oakdale, he had already made several attempts on his life. Although he had only been engaged for a month, the loss had made him inconsolable. It tied into too many old, old hurts with such a burden on his mind that he could not rise above it.

Jacob came into the program as half the other patients were being discharged. This left me in need of a roommate, and we were paired together based on the simple fact we were both male. "Jacob" was likable. Slow to speak, but invariably kind and insightful when he did. He was polite, but definitely withdrawn. In groups, he would often cry, and be very demonstrative with his emotions. And although it was slow going, as it was with many, he began to participate in meals, and all of the events that comprised a complete day.

During the course of a patient's week, they met in individual therapy with their counselor as a part of the program. Jacob had come into our room crying after his therapy session. We sat down on the edge of his bed, and talked about how the day had been for him.

He opened up, and began to talk about how isolated he had been from genuine affection during his life. This began with his parents being very emotionally abusive and distant. He said he could recall hearing the words "I love you" a total of four or five times during his childhood. These rare words were combined with moments of abuse at the hands of his father, and it made for a very cold and scary young life.

However, Jacob had managed to get through high school, and enlist in the armed forces. He was training to be a medic, and said he really enjoyed the work. In this training, he had met a young lady named Emma. As he began to relate this to me, he almost sounded hopeful.

"Reece," Jacob began, dropping down on my bed. Can we talk about this for a few minutes? I want to tell you about my anger management session I just had." I liked anger management. It was one of the few activities which brought about a visceral experience. The idea was to throw a ball of clay at a wall while focusing on either releasing anger or empowering the self. The rhythm of the bang of the clay on the wall, and the smell of the wet putty in your hands made for a multi-sensory experience.

"I was just throwing in anger management," Jacob said. "I hated it! Every one of the anger statements made me feel sad, rather than mad at Emma. I am trying to feel anger, but all I feel is loss—this incredible loss."

At the time, I had no words of wisdom for Jacob. It somehow gets around the unit fairly quickly when a therapist is among the patients, and I was soon the target of numerous questions. Jacob wasn't pushy. He just really needed to talk to someone, and I was trying to fulfill that need.

Jacob continued asking questions based on the great "Why?" of his life. Why him? Why now? Why had she left? These were mysteries that ripped at his very being. He shed tears as he recounted abuses and isolation. He was in a dark place far from any Light.

I had to get a shower, but I promised we would talk more later. When I finished my shower, and was getting dressed, Jacob left the room. I assumed he was walking to the Sanctuary. However, he took a right turn out of the room to walk down the hall.

Before any one could do anything to stop him, Jacob launched himself into a full run down the hall toward one of the load bearing poles that ran between the floors. The pole was huge, with a circumference of about seven feet. Jacob ran full speed into the pole. It was all over in a few seconds. And a ripple of fear went through the entire group.

The staff surrounded Jacob within seconds. The nurses flew into action, checking vitals, and one shouted for a 911 call. It seemed to take forever for the EMTs to arrive. They took over for the staff, and administered CPR. As they rolled Jacob out of our lives forever, my spirit stirred, and I prayed for Jacob. I also prayed for myself. I knew what awaited Jacob if he had been successful, and I was not surprised to find myself feeling a bit envious.

Chapter Twenty Seven – The Business of Healing

For the next several days, I continued to make some strides, avoided sad situations, and did my best to keep from having to receive CPR. I thrived on a combination of reading, and working the cognitive therapy Dr. Z. offered.

Cognitive theory is a counseling theory. It basically says we can change our emotions and reactions to situations we encounter by examining our belief system about things we experience. If you know anything about computers, it is basically akin to the idea of changing software on your computer. Let's say you have Word, a popular processing program, installed on your computer. Every time you write something, your computer writes down the words in the Word program. Now think about what would happen if your Word software was broken, and it only wrote down every other word you typed. You would become frustrated, and you would want to change from Word to Fast Writer, so your computer would catch all the words you wrote down. You change the software by uninstalling Word, and installing Fast Writer. Suddenly, your computer is working just fine again, and is happily recording every word you wrote. Problem solved.

Well, cognitive theory kind of works along these same lines. The theory holds that when we aren't getting the results we want, we need to uninstall the old program, install a new program, and a see if it works better for us. Our "program", or software, is our mind-self's current statement. Most of us have a hard time with some of our mind-self's statements. For example, when we meet new people, we may feel very anxious. Or, we may assume the person will not want to be our friend.

These feelings, reacting to the situation of meeting a new person, come from our previous experiences in dealing with new people. Somewhere in the past, a similar situation did not go well. Perhaps someone poked fun at you while you were attending a social event when you were a child. Or a parent made a hateful statement about you. Whatever the situation, we learned to react in a negative way to the situation of meeting new people.

However, just like writing with Word, and not getting all the words down in the computer, we are acting out and not getting the right beliefs and emotional responses. Consider changing that software. Our software is our mind-self. It is the common knowledge of all things we have ever learned. It processes every signal from the outside world. Now we have to get rid of our Word program, and go get Fast Writer for our computer to react better—more efficiently. Cognitive theory says this can be done by thinking of new reactions and planting them in our minds. So, when the situation of meeting new people presents itself, we can react differently.

Among my best experiences at Oakdale, were my sessions with Dr. Z. Although I would be hard-pressed to recall everything we talked about in the sessions, they did reach me in a way that was assuring and powerful. During his session, Dr. Z. would guide me with simple questions beginning with, "Tell me about what is going on, and whom you live with?" From there, he would have me explore past experiences, and how they related to my expression of emotions and present behaviors.

I had three primary demons to deal with during these sessions. First, was the sickening abuse I experienced at the hands of my Uncle Tom. The second was the tragedy of the nerve damage and the resulting chronic pain from the botched surgery. Finally, I had to deal with crossing twice—over to heaven, and then back to this life again. All of these events had been driving a host of unreasonable beliefs for me when I arrived at Oakdale, including:

- God hated me and wished me to suffer.
- I was not good enough for people to love me.
- God wanted to judge me and condemn me.
- I was unworthy of having good things for my life.
- I was worthless and could be used by anyone.

These are common, irrational beliefs of survivors of various types of abuse. These beliefs come from deep self-statements from the mind-self. What is required for healing is for the mind-self to change its thinking.

However, that is not a simple matter. I began to wonder how the brain, that could only collect information, could exercise enough control over itself to "simply change its thinking." This would be akin to a leopard simply changing its spots. The word "simply" was dropped from the equation, as day after day I tried to use the cognitive approach.

I decided there was something missing in that approach. However, it was an approach that would bring me from feeling like a minus ten to feeling like a positive three. But the road ahead was still a long and winding one!

Twenty-Eight – Where's the Spirit?

Cognitive therapy, as advanced by Dr. Z., never tapped into the spiritual side of things, and it was my spiritual-self that needed the focus. I needed to hold up, in front of a mirror, what had happened to me, to see what was left from the crossing to learn. What was left to share? What was left to apply? One cannot visit paradise and not be overwhelmed by the return. One cannot visit paradise and not desire to be back within its fold.

My life felt like an unfinished path—a driveway reaching only halfway to a garage. Spirit-self is as important as body-self and mind-self. I would not learn that lesson until I began work with a very talented therapist named Suzette Doescher.

Somehow it seemed like just days had gone by, but in fact, three weeks had passed, and I was ready to leave the Trauma Unit at Oakdale. I had been stabilized, and was now ready to transfer out to their day program. There I would begin working with Suzette. But, there was one last day to complete on the unit.

I had become very, very close to the people who shared the Trauma Unit with me during my stay. Even the staff members and I had made bonds that would be missed. And the patients had changed my life through their learning and sharing. Dr. Z. had prepared me to ask the important questions. The institutional food had left me ten pounds lighter. The Sanctuary had turned me into a smoker. The coffee had made me a caffeine junkie. All things considered though, I dreaded saying goodbye my final day.

The morning I was to leave, we began AM group according to routine. However, one-by-one, the patients, when asked how they felt, echoed "confident," and added, "for Reece!" When asked what the goal was, everyone on the unit answered, "hug Reece," or "say goodbye to Reece." Even the staff leaders echoed the sentiment.

I was touched. Here were a group of people, all suffering from their own personal horror stories, and they were focused on letting me know I was loved. We had spent three weeks together laughing, crying, and just surviving. We had seen some come, and then be released to go home, and still others went on to long-term care facilities. We had shared it all, and I will always be grateful that my personal stories were not the worst of those heard on the unit. However, I do weep for those who had been so badly treated by life that my story paled in comparison. I left with these new beliefs stirring in me. They were not yet truths because I had not yet become aware of the spirit-self burning within me. But I wrote these down in my journal in the last hours I was on the unit.

- I am loved.
- Bad things have happened, but they were beyond my control.
- I can control how I react to things.
- There are good people in the world.
- There is a God Who loves me.

- I have all of the strength I need to change my own life.

With those final words woven like a tapestry of humanity at Oakdale, I would like to introduce Suzette, a true agent of change in my life.

Chapter Twenty Nine - The Great Suzette Doescher

Suzette had escaped New Orleans in the wake of Katrina. The horrible storm had robbed her of her home and her possessions. I am truly thankful it did not rob her spirit. Suzette arrived in Texas with essentially the clothes on her back, and her license to practice as a social worker in Texas.

Suzette was a powerhouse of a woman. Standing only 5'6", with a head of silver hair, one would never guess this would be the vessel God would use to put me in touch with my spirit-self in such an amazing way!

Suzette was, as were most of the counselors I knew at Oakdale, a devotee of the cognitive theories, with a few exceptions.

"You have to replace the truths, truths with a little t, with Truths with a capital T," she began in our first session.

With those words, something clicked in the back of my mind. There was something so simple about the way she talked about truths versus Truths.

It was her word for my decision to seek bigger, better beliefs in the place of smaller, destructive beliefs that had led me to my troubles in life. What were some of those beliefs I was holding at the time I entered Oakdale's program?

God was angry with me on some level and did not want me in paradise.

I was unlovable.

I was in severe pain, and nothing could be done about it.

My family did not accept me.

I was incapable of making my own living.

I was dependent on my father for my livelihood.

These little "t" truths were out for a firestorm of challenges and redirections during the next few weeks. I was going to be picking apart these beliefs, discovering where and why they had come to exist.

The Day Program at Oakdale was located on a floor beneath the Trauma Unit. Thankfully, it was completely free of any signs alerting one to the fact you were on a "restricted unit." The Day Program was not based on the "Thou Shalt Not " theory, and allowed full access to all areas at all times. It was designed to move patients from the safety and fulltime support of the Trauma Unit, and prepare them for return to life in the real world.

The Day Program continued to be a structured setting. The group of five to ten people would gather in a comfortable little room in the Lane Unit. None of us knew quite what to expect the first morning on the "outside." We were giggling, and drinking obscene amounts of caffeine. We walked outside, looked-up to where the Sanctuary of nicotine hovered over the lawn below, and taunted the ones remaining on the "inside."

Essentially, we were claiming the rights of the "outties!" We were bandaged—had earned our patches pasted-over our emotional wounds. We would watch those wounds form scars during our time in the Day Program.

Guiding us on this path was Suzette. There were five of us, and Suzette gave it her all to keep each one feeling as if she were focused on that one only. Her size belied her ability to fly from person-to-person and back to the chalkboard. She threw titles of books at us as if hurling rocks at our old beliefs. She diagrammed, she pleaded, and she assigned homework. For a woman who had lost everything just months before, she was an amazingly effective therapist!

Suzette also had a distinctive personality that led some to love her, and some to be less than enthusiastic about her. It was "love me or hate me," and she really did seem undaunted by which way clients would go. She had a job to do. And, she did it with the self-assurance of someone who was not only well-practiced, but who passionately believed in the "big T" Truths.

Her passion for this belief helped my spirit-self awaken my mind-self. My mind-self was still holding fast to old beliefs from the experience of sexual abuse by Uncle Tom, the physical abuse by a stepfather, a crippling injury from a botched surgery, and finally my great disappointment at being sent back from the Source. As you can imagine, Suzette had her work cut out for her!

It would be a very powerful three weeks. Few would make it to the end of the prescribed program. Especially those with DID, and various other severe personality disorders.

Those of us, however, who responded to cognitive therapy, blossomed. Not only would I flourish with the cognitive therapy, but I would find my spirit-self as well. I would find it sitting on a badly worn brown sofa, somewhere in the underbelly of the Trauma Unit. God would use a woman named Suzette. This is how He began bringing Reece Manley back to his intended work for good.

Part of the routine of the Day Program included signing-in daily, and filling-out a brief form on how our night had gone. We rated our depression, anxiety, and more, for the purpose of creating great reams of paperwork. Besides, it created more work for those like Miss K. in the front office! She and her plastic pearls probably curse me to this day.

One morning I wrote down, "I had a nightmare about my crossing." It was the first time I mentioned my near death experience to Suzette, although I'm sure she had read my file with its carefully documented notes from counseling. One day, she pulled me aside during the break. "Break" being the official term for the mad rush of nicotine addicts who would shove each other to the ground to get ahead. We lit up 15 feet from the building. We must have looked like a sad bunch "fixing our habits" like our lives depended on it.

I was focused on pulling out a lighter, a pack of cigarettes, and extrapolating one said cigarette from the pack in a single fluid motion. I almost missed Suzette's words. "We need to talk after classes today," she said. It didn't register with me that I was about to have a very important discussion that day. I believe God sends us thousands, or even millions of such little moments to tell our spirit-self to listen. That message got through with a tap from Above.

"I'm sorry, Suzette. What did you say?"

"We need to talk a few minutes after we finish classes today, " she repeated. I felt my brow furl with the thought of having to delay the demand for nicotine. "Don't worry," Suzette said, "I know better than to fight nicotine addiction. I just want to speak with you after classes end today."

The group went quickly out the door, and to the designated smoking patio. Patients, wait, no, we were now clients. Clients like to gossip about the goings-on at Oakdale, and I was happy to contribute to the groups fodder for focus during the next twenty minutes. The gossip went around and around with puffs of smoke, and gulps of caffeine interrupting the flow. Before we knew it, the twenty minutes had gone by, and we were making our way to the rest of the day's classes.

At the end of the day, I sought out Suzette in the little office she shared with another therapist at the end of the hall. She motioned for me, and I took a seat on the chair directly in front of her desk. She held a piece of paper in front of her and studied it. With dread, I recognized it as my sign-in sheet for the day.

"You know, Reece," she began, "This is your key. This is the thing that is going to make it easier for you than for anyone else in this group. You know why that is?" I was stunned. Not only did I not know why that was so, but I didn't know how she could say such a thing. I was here to recover from my crossing. In my mind, recovery meant to put something behind you. To forget about it. To put it in its place, and not dwell upon it. And, here was the woman whose opinion I most valued in terms of healing help, telling me a piece of paper was my "key."

"No, Suzette, I don't know why that is," I responded.

She dropped the sheet, looked over her reading glasses at me, and studied me for a moment. This was one of her favorite poses to strike with me. Her eyes seemed to be underscored by her reading glasses for emphasis. It was as if what she said **was going to be very important**. "You already have a capital T," she said.

She paused, and a grin played over her face. She looked very much like a six-year-old who had shared the most precious secret in the universe with her little brother. "A capital T as in capital T for Truth."

She laid down the paper, allowed the grin to subside, took off her reading glasses, and laid them down. All this she did without taking her eyes off of mine.

"What would you think about us working together after I'm done with the Day Program, Suzette?" My mouth said the words without any permission on my part! I remember thinking someone behind me said the words, and I started to turn my head before I recognized my own voice. Occasionally the spirit-self does reach out and take over the body-self!

Suzette smiled broadly and returned, "I thought you might ask that." She hauled up her scheduling book stuffed with sticky notes, and shuffled through it. "Looks like you can have Thursdays at 11:00 AM. Does that sound good to you?"'

No! I thought! That certainly does not sound good. I don't want to know the big T's in life.

I was satisfied with knowing the little "t" truths. The simple, small, easy to follow "t's" that only required me to follow a certain list of rules resulting in an acceptable life. The last thing I wanted to do was add big, life-altering "Ts" into my life. Absolutely not!

"Yes. That sounds great." Who said that?

I opened my mouth to correct the statement, but found myself being cut off quickly.

"Great," said Suzette. That's it. Oh, and your time is about up here at the Day Program. We're looking at discharge Tuesday, so I'll be seeing you next on our first appointment on Thursday." She set her schedule book back into place on the pile of paperwork. *What just happened here? Did time shift?* "Anything else," Suzette asked?

I found my hand digging quite frantically in my right pocket, and performing its cigarette retrieval trick. I was set-up with the great Suzette Doescher, LCSW as my primary therapist. Oh what a difference a few seconds make!

In retrospect, Suzette was exactly who I needed. I believe the Source moves people in and out of our lives when both parties can benefit from it. If you ever find yourself wondering why a major relationship just seemed to pop into your life, you can be certain your spirit-self has been working with the Source.

I met Suzette for our first session the following Thursday. Her office was hard to find, and I arrived puffing from the brisk walk over each floor of the building. The sign on the door read "Practical Wisdom," and Suzette's name was duly noted below the plaque.

Our first session began the way I had initiated sessions with my clients, "So, tell me what's going on with you?" It was very weird for me to be on the other side of the counseling chair! "After all, you know it's all connected so any place you want to start is fine." And, so it began with a simple question that would lead to a healing relationship that would bring me to an emotional plus ten!

The sessions with Suzette were inspired. It turns out the Truths with the capital T came to me quickly through my work with Suzette. She focused on the beliefs I held, and we examined each one carefully. As we would go through the beliefs, I would keep turning back to my time in the presence of the Source. There, I would find Truth. I challenged beliefs that would not stand up to what I knew to be capital Ts.

It was hard work emotionally. I spoke at length about the terror of being at the mercy of Tom—the feeling of being used and dirty. The feeling that came when I was crying, alone, a young child trying to hide the evidence of the rape I had just endured lest someone find out. Tom had instilled a belief in me that love was hurtful and manipulative. In the face of the Creator, I found no such evidence. Instead, I found that love is gentle and kind.

We delved into the beliefs created by the beatings of a stepfather. He would deliver unspeakable terror and pain upon me, and I watched in horror as he did the same to my younger brother. The belief that I was powerless was challenged and replaced. There is all power in the Source, and it is a loving, healing power.

We examined the horrible aftermath of the gastric bypass surgery. It had left me with damage to nerve cells that had no idea how to heal themselves. They call out their injury 24/7/365. Unending in their assault of pain, they are simply damaged tissue. They are not proof that God is angry with me. During the crossing, there was no pain, only comfort and great joy.

Each time an old belief was changed; my spirit-self stirred, and made the connection to the mind-self. I don't know how else to explain it. There was a Divine power at work as I changed each belief. The power to change was not coming from my physical-self. It remained in pain, and limited me. The power did not come from my mind-self. My emotions only winced and writhed under the memories generated by the storage of the mind-self's vivid ability to recall happenings.

If neither the body-self, nor the mind-self was working, what was working on my behalf?

I began to voraciously study spirituality. I considered all of the major religions. Some words I found to be untruthful, even though they were taken for truth by millions. But, one theme in almost every tome I reviewed, pointed out that mankind is eternal. Rather, some part of the whole person is eternal. However, some things written in the religious works I studied, directly challenged the Truth about the Creator as I knew Him. He loves us, and He does so through a direct connection to our spirit-self. I suspected that some of the words were conceived by man rather than inspired by God. The God I knew was fully powerful, loving, gentle, and kind. This was a big Truth for me on the road to dispelling old beliefs.

Any old belief could be challenged! Suzette taught me that through examining each belief. However, in order to challenge the belief, we must first articulate it. Whether we write it down in a journal, create a poem, write a song—the old belief must be stated so it can be challenged. Making the belief concrete, so it can be effectively challenged and changed, was like taking a checklist to the grocery so nothing important could be overlooked. Yes, there it was, right on the list—a dozen eggs I needed for the soufflé! I made the business of concretizing a daily task, and soon it became as simple as ticking-off the list at the grocery.

I practiced this step over and over as I brought out each old belief, and challenged it with my spirit-self in connection with the Creator, rather than with my mind-self. While the mind-self is a brilliant, shining diamond of accomplishment, (more powerful than we yet know,) it is limited in comparison to the spirit-self. Yes, the mind-self is limited to past knowledge. It is not capable of conceiving unique challenges of future knowledge.

Whatever action or reaction we have to a place, person, or situation—no matter how logical we try to be, our mind-self is affected by every similar past experience; it makes a judgment, and then reacts based on past knowledge—repeated experiences. These experiences go all the way back to birth.

Not surprisingly, the mind-self has written millions of scripts to handle every situation, which has been experienced. Each time it adds to the little truths. This truth becomes a belief over time, and the mind-self automatically reacts to any given situation by playing back this mind-self experiences tape!

Without the spirit-self, we cannot effectively change our reactions, emotions, or behaviors. We cannot effectively love ourselves or love others. Without the spirit-self, we can't realize our full potential because we are living life by two-thirds of who we really are. Why would anyone want to live in such a limited way—missing one-third of what is rightfully his or hers through the Source? Talk about a handicap! Yes, I was spiritually handicapped, and so was mankind—hobbling around with two-thirds potential on a daily basis!

I began to bring out more and more old beliefs, and for each one I tried, I allowed my spirit-self to test it as true or false. Each time, my spirit-self was able to give a new Truth to the situation.

I worked with Suzette once a week for four months. At the beginning, the work was slow. I had to face all of my graduate-level training in counseling, and my doctoral work in human development. All of the documents on my wall, testifying I was an expert on mind issues, were working against any true change.

Chapter Thirty – Coming to Power

As time went on, it became easier. I developed my connection to my spirit-self to the point that it was an ever-present part of my daily life. When new situations arose, or an old one changed, my mind-self would actually wait to receive the consciousness of my spirit-self to act upon the situation. My spirit-self would seek out its connection to the Creator for inspiration, information, and structure. And power—such incredible power I found in the connection to the Source.

There is nothing—no belief that cannot be overcome by the Source. And our spirit-selves give a direct, intimate connection to the Source.

At the end of our time together, I had accomplished many things. By embracing the study of spirituality and guided prayer work, I was eventually able to obtain ordination as a minister through Many Paths Ministry. Because I believed other than Christians were destined for paradise, I could not be ordained through the denomination of my childhood. I had learned during my time with the Source, that black or white, Republican or Democrat, gay or straight, one religion or another, did not determine our acceptance or rejection by the Source. What did matter was Love.

After I obtained ordination, I began to reach out to new clients. Instead of offering clinical counseling, I ministered to them as a professional pastoral counselor. This allows me to see clients through the role of clergy. In this way, I was free to speak about the spirit, prayer, and Truth that exists in the spirit-self.

Suzette and I came to the end of our supportive relationship. She had lovingly pressured me to go forward bravely. She had encouraged the Truth of love, and prodded me to learn, read, pray, and challenge old beliefs over and over.

On the day of our last session, it was difficult for me to break away. We wept together as I tried to thank her for all she had done, but my words, though heart-felt, could never be sufficient. Suzette sent me forth with these words, "Reece, you have come so far on your path. Keep walking it. You are loved. You know the Truth. Keep to your path, and your path alone. That's where Truth is for you."

I'm still walking my path, Suzette!

Chapter Thirty One - What I've Learned

I lost the knowledge I had gained in the Crossing, however, I was left with insights and wisdom from being in the presence of the One.

Inside the Crossing...

The Light was overwhelming. I had run a marathon in a matter of seconds—like climbing to the peak of Everest in a minute, I pulsed with an incredible energy overreaching any joy or love I had ever known. Pulsing, yet still radiant even during the recess of the pulse. The knowledge was accumulating so quickly into my awareness from my connection, not only to the Creator but also through the connections to the other millions of lights, that my awareness was beyond belief.

Each of us, each little orb, was as gloriously brilliant as the Creator, simply on a smaller scale. Smaller, but no less loved or accepted or celebrated, was my light. I was larger than some others. We were each unique in the combination of energy and love and joy that was being celebrated. Each spirit-self connected to the Creator strongly, and still connected to each other to a lesser degree. It was a network of knowledge, wisdom, and insight into every discipline of study, but also a network into every positive emotion ever felt. In this great network, I danced, pulsed, celebrated, and absorbed.

To this day, I still wake-up from dreaming of those few moments on the other side where everything knowable is known, and everything joyous is tangible. How little I brought back with me as my spirit-self was lovingly exiled, but only for a short time. It was necessary for me to wait until it was my true time to go home to heaven.

I still receive inspirations of Truth, and hear the Spirit of Wisdom I brought back with me.

One of these inspirations was lovingly nurtured through a path the Creator gave to me: the opportunity to approach and challenge others.

It has led to the writing of this book. I hope this work touches at least one person with the understanding that they are loved, accepted, and perfect in the spirit-self through its connection to the Source. If just one person out there stops hating self or others, then my pain, my efforts, my challenges have not been in vain.

Another inspiration came about through the art of helping others—one that nurtured me through my recovery from the miracle of my crossing. I continually seek and work through new challenges with a proven approach which I call **"Spirit Thinking."** Proven one client at a time, and one session at a time through my practice, it has been beneficial to helping others formulate new beliefs from Truths. I believe it will be a wonderful work for anyone considering a change in his or her life based on the power of the spirit-self.

You don't have to change religions, attend a different church, join an organization, or stop carrying your favorite icons—as a matter of fact, you only give up any ill-conceived beliefs within your old mind-self, and move on to new beliefs formulated on Truth. In rebuilding a computer, the technician reprograms, updates, adds new software as needed, and then runs a Norton full-system scan! This is what **"Spirit Thinking"** does—it puts you at the controls of your mind-self motherboard! See below to learn more about the **Spirit Thinking** approach to healing.

Spirit Thinking: Your 30 Day Guide to an Enlightenment. This guide and workbook by Dr. Reece Manley is designed to help you be your best now through Spirit Thinking!

 Go online to order at http://www.SpiritThinking.Net.

Part Two

Ten Questions About my Journey to Heaven

From: *Crossing Twice: Answers from the Source*

As I continue what has become a small ministry of spreading the great news of God's love and compassion for all people, I have received a number of questions about my crossing over. Many questions are often repeated, giving me clues to what readers most want to know and understand about my crossing over. I pray my responses will bring clarification and insight.

Is Death Painful?

For me, and for most others I have researched, the answer is <u>no</u>. Crossing is never a painful experience. For me, it was just the opposite. It was the complete release from pain. The complete absence of the pain which had plagued my life for eight years; it simply vanished as I entered the cool gray mist of the first stage of the crossing.

As I relive the moment I have to smile. I smile because I know one day I'll have that experience again! Today, my chronic pain is a constant, dark companion, always fighting for my hopes and optimism. In the crossing, though, the pain was instantly gone.

I believe as soon as we begin the death crossing, we are immediately freed from our body-self. We simply exit as if we were getting out of a car from which we have suddenly found the door. I found a door which had been hidden all my life, and which is hidden to me again now until my next crossing.

Simply opening a door. I knew I had to move "forward" as if I were called to a place far away. I didn't have to do anything other than move forward. It was completely comfortable, completely painless, and completely free of any kind of unpleasant experiences.

Do We See God?

Yes, we do see God. It is an awe-inspiring experience that leaves one trembling. My first vision of God was the incredibly bright Light. It was a Light so intense it should have been painful. So powerfully bright I should have hidden my eyes. So strong I should have been knocked to my knees (like Saul on the road to Damascus, who later became the Apostle Paul of the New Testament,) and I might have done that, except I had no knees!

I had no eyes, no knees, no arms, no feet. God was a great Light—so great was His expanse that it seemed to stretch beyond planets. It should have been terrifying in some way, but it was only reassuring. I knew I was in the right place!

As I began to adjust to what was happening around me, I was suddenly struck with what seemed a physical bolt, a link directly to my heart, which filled me with the most wonderful compassion and love, the likes of which I had never known.

Compassion is such a wonderful, but limited word when trying to convey the absolute love you experience in the Presence. Even though the Creator knows all of your flaws, all of your deepest secrets in an instant, they are suddenly whisked away like leaves on a fall wind!

The fact that God loved me was so incredible that my mind was having a hard time fathoming it at first. The Creator of the Universe was taking a moment out of eternity to tell me I was his beloved child! My heart softened, and any resistance I ever had against believing in a loving Creator was gone in a flash. It did not matter who I had been or what I had done in my life. I had done great things, and I had done small things, I had committed great sins, and I had committed small sins. But none of it made a difference.

The complete focus of God's love and compassion was upon me in an embrace beyond what we humans can ever give. Another human will not love you in your earthly life the way God loves you. Nor will you be called to return love in the same way as your heart will long for the Creator. Our connections to our parents, our siblings, our children are all wonderful experiences for us to know on earth. They are among the greatest of the gifts we get to know in this lifetime. But, they are but a petal on the greatest bouquet of blossoms of God's love, compassion, and peace. With that one jolt – that split second – not only did I know I had "seen" God, but I knew God had seen me!

What About Loved Ones Who Have Passed-On?

We do see our loved ones from earth after we cross over! Our deceased loved ones from this life, and from lives past, are awaiting us in Heaven. However, they don't look exactly like we remember them.

I didn't recognize anyone until the bolt of light directly from God welcomed me into Heaven. With that embrace, I suddenly became aware of all things. For a human mind, such a revelation would have been impossible. But, I suddenly knew multitudes of people instantly, intimately, and completely. I had access to all of their accumulated knowledge. I knew the story of each of their lives. As the Spirit connected us, it was abundantly clear where my loved ones were, and within seconds I was surrounded by them, dancing and bobbing. They were thriving in their spirit forms! We rejoiced as we joined each other in a group with ever-expanding connections. As God's Spirit made all the connections, each one would come from the far ends of the celestial realm. I saw my Uncle Bob, an old prankster while he had been alive, was perfectly restored. I saw my beloved Uncle Wayne, who had been robbed of life by Lou Gehrig's Disease or ALS. He was strong and restored on the other side—full of the light and life he had when I'd known him.

Then there were the others. The dark persons from my past. I am pleased to say God's Love and compassion extends beyond so far, that my best efforts at forgiveness as a human were humbly broken for a new model of Divine compassion. Still some of these dark ones remained separated from the Light. They were among us like gray stones in a riverbed. They had chosen not to accept the love and power of God. Though we could see them, there was no connection, no communication, and no acknowledgement in either direction. They were not "with us" in the Light of God.

What Does Heaven Look Like?

It is amazing how many times I'm asked about how heaven looked at my crossing. Jesus spent a great deal of his ministry speaking in parables, and using metaphors to describe His Father, Heaven, and His impending death and resurrection. During the latter explanation, Jesus refers to His body as a "temple," that if torn down, would be rebuilt within three days. This is just one example of Jesus' use of metaphor about a building that is not a building at all, but a metaphor for His body, the house of the Holy Spirit of God.

The lack of physical structure in Heaven may be quite a surprise for those who were expecting great houses and golden streets based on the words in the Bible. That doesn't mean the Bible is wrong, or that my experience wasn't valid. In my case there were no physical trappings, as we know them on earth. Although, I know it would not be beyond the power of the Creator to make Heaven appear like earth if that were necessary for the comfort of the residents of Heaven.

No, I did not see a single physical structure in heaven. Yet, it was the most powerful, beautiful place I had ever been. There were golden ropes of light passing from the great Source to each of the celestial residents. The golden light of the Source fell upon everything. The stars stretched-out before us in what seemed millions and millions of miles, while we danced among each other in perfect adoration, peace, and power. Each resident's "rope" connected directly to the Source, each outshone the brightest lights one can imagine.

I do believe Heaven physically exists in a different place, or on a different plane. It is a supernatural place in a supernatural location. Somewhere in the vastness of space and time, exists the Source. And the space within the scope of the direct Light of the Source is Heaven. While there were, it seemed, millions and millions of souls there, we were not crowded. We were unconcerned about "houses" or "streets." They simply had no meaning to us, and we had no need for them.

I know there have been those who have visited the other side, and have seen houses of gold, and streets of gold. There may be some reason the Source was presenting such things.

I, myself, was expecting a great golden gate, clouds with angels on them, and a thousand other preconceived comforts. What I found, instead, was the most beautiful, peaceful place. A place that was greater than a city made of gold or great houses built to accommodate souls. There was no need for walls. There was no need for gold because the Light was more valuable than any precious metal.

What Do You Hear in Heaven?

I heard symphonies and orchestras, songs and praises, and voices of the residents of Heaven. Yes, Heaven has sounds—sounds of pure peace!

Sound is, of course, one of our physical senses, so I must begin by saying that I heard with my spirit ears, not my physical ears. So, it is a hearing one is not used to experiencing. The closest example I can offer for the sounds of heaven, is that it is voice and sound that plays inside your mind. Very few of us run a speaking dialogue of, "okay, now I'm going to the coffee maker, oops...don't step on the dog but do step over the dog, dog that's kind of a funny word, dog. Dog. Og. Fog. Ah, Foglifter coffee! That's what I was going for—coffee," If we did give voice to the running dialogue going on in our heads, very few of us would pass for sane! However, you know what I mean when I say "inner voice."

When one is standing in heaven, one has no ears, yet one hears. Only at the beginning of the transformation is the silence startling. When I first started my crossing, one of the signals to me that something different was happening, was the complete void—the silence. As the machines of the hospital faded behind me, the cool, gray mist began to enfold me, and my mind grew calm. I distinctly remember the rhythm of the ventilator breathing for me. It was making this incredulously loud hum while a monitor pinged some information out to the ICU staff. As I left the room in the first stages of the afterlife, the quiet embraced me like a warm blanket. It was a remarkably peaceful, comforting silence.

As the "lifepoints," a term I use to refer to the review of my life, began to sharpen, I heard things in a new way. All the voices and noise were being generated by the inner voice. However, it was not this timid, reserved inner voice we imagine the inner voice to be, but it was huge and powerful. It was full of detail from my collected experiences, my knowledge, and focus I had had at those points in my life.

From the lifepoints, sounds were familiar and enhanced. Voices were more detailed, conveying information about emotional states and the speaker's intentions, more than I should have ever known. The sounds in one lifepoint were from a cold snowy day, and I could hear individual snowflakes fall. They made a little tinkle when they landed on other flakes.

As the lifepoints faded, I again entered into silence. It would be the last time I would experience things through the familiarity of my physical being. Instead I passed through that great crimson field, and stood a long way off from a very bright Light. There was total silence for a moment. Then, a choir. Alternatively, rather, voices singing the most excited, most upbeat, most jubilant song I ever heard. The voices were singing in a thousand different languages. At first, the sound was confusing. I could tell it was glorious, but it made no sense. Then, just as suddenly, I realized the voices were indeed singing a language I did understand. Or, rather, they were singing a thousand different languages I could understand! First the choral voices, then the sounds of great joy being played on the sweetest instruments. Joy—Incredible joy! I was surrounded by the sounds of celebration. I was literally riding wave after wave of happiness. Then the song changed, and I began to "feel" the sounds. The sounds became a great welling-up of emotions—I could feel Love through the music!

How Do We Look in Heaven?

We are beautiful beyond belief. Nevertheless, there is quite a difference in how we look there, and how we appear on earth. One of the most powerful experiences in my crossing over into the next life was the transformation of my body. No, it was more than a transformation; it was a "transfiguration" of the flesh of the body, and the structure of mind into the Light of Spirit-self.

As I stood on the edge of the realm of Heaven and became aware of the Creator as a Great Light, I also realized I had no form resembling a body!

I was pondering this in the back of my mind, I believe, when the first bolt from the Creator struck me. The Father shared with me the most powerful compassion, love, peace, and strength. As I absorbed these offerings, almost feeling as if I would explode if the love became any more intense, I noticed a white glow outside the field of my vision.

As I was given wisdom from the Father, I instinctively braced for the bolt, but instead of being depleted, I glowed more brightly! I could tell I had a form, but it was a glowing, spherical shape! I was perhaps six feet in diameter, and I shimmered with Light from the Creator, and from my own spirit-self. The Light spread outward to infinity.

When it came time for me to move throughout the realm, I did so with such speed that all things blurred. I was drawn to others, called to celebrate with other Spirits. We were sharing joy and ecstasy! Each soul loved me completely. Each person shared their lives with me as I shared mine with them. We laughed like old friends do when they are reunited after a long while. I did not know how I knew some of them, but I shared memories and joy with them nonetheless. Some were complete strangers, yet we greeted each other in love, acceptance, peace, and praise for the Creator.

We are beautiful in heaven! We are forever young and learning. There is no way to describe the stunning awe of looking out on multitudes of people, all made in the form of the Creator. The beauty of the light between the Creator and each of us, was striking beyond description. We aren't all spirit models of Brad Pitt and Angelina Jolie; we are much more beautiful as spirits!

Are There Angels in Heaven?

Multitudes of angels inhabit the celestial realm! Some "appear" in human form. Racing from the edges of Heaven to do the Creator's bidding, they fly at dizzying speeds. Sometimes, they were smaller bright lights, little orbs of intense power. They buzzed around the Creator, and actually entered into the Sphere of the Creator. Going within the boundaries of the Creator's Light. They were mysteries to us.

Although they exerted and extended great love to all of us who were God's children, the angels were different and separate. It was clear they were beings with purpose, and the Creator gave plans to them. I believe God creates each one of us for some Divine purpose. Angels were created separately from man, for different reasons and purposes. They race about without free will, following the will of the Divine.

While on earth, I experienced the intervention of angels twice. One time I was with my mother; we were driving in

Lubbock, Texas. A car wreck happened very near us. The crashing and crunching of metal was a terrifying sound. I thought surely there would be a fatality. And then, out of the corner of my eye I saw something racing past us to the scene. My mother and I both smelled the scent of roses. The air was heavy with the smell of pungent roses. Angels had been near us, and we were at peace knowing they were at work helping the survivors of the accident.

The second time I had an angel experience was on a rainy day in September 1998. I was having a bad day. It had started-out bad when I overslept for work, and worsened as I rushed down to the car.

I discovered someone had bashed-in the side window, and stolen the radio and my portfolio from the passenger side. I drove to work with water spilling into my car. The day did not get much better. It was the day of trading, and I lost over $55,000 for my company. My boss did not think this was funny, and I went home with a docked paycheck. On the way home, a large Semi truck decided to scoot over into my lane. However, he had not seen me at all. He began his lane change;

I honked my horn, desperate to stop him. There was the crunch of metal on metal as I braked hard and he sped ahead. The car behind me barely had time to respond without crashing into me from behind. The left front tire has been ruined in the collision. I had come within inches of losing my life. As I changed the tire in heavy traffic, with more pelting rain coming down, I was decidedly not a happy camper, and I uttered "Fine, God. Don't care!"

At home, I headed for the shower. Once robed and scrambling for some semblance of supper, I noticed the red light on my Caller ID box was blinking. I stopped to scroll through the messages. There was one call, and my heart changed rhythm! At 5:15 PM, right when I would have been having my accident, the following call had come in. "Guardian Angel 777-777-7777". No message, except the obvious.

It could have been a spoof? Surely, there was an explanation for the number, my rational mind-self suggested. However, for my spirit-self, the explanation was that I had had a very busy angel who had kept my bad day from being my last day! We've all had such experiences we cannot explain in some rational way.

Is There a Hell?

This topic is one that is bound to raise great debate. However, I saw no Hell, and had no experience with it. Gauging by the Creator's boundless love and compassion, I do not believe there is such a place where He would send his children.

Nevertheless, mankind has been given a terribly powerful quality – Free Will. There are those who choose, for whatever reason, to completely refuse to accept the Creator's love and compassion.

In the celestial realm, among those of us who were glowing brightly and dancing in celebration, were the darker ones. The darker spheres did not have a link to the Creator, or to us, not even to each other. They were totally and completely cut off from God and others. Although God's love shone throughout us all, these souls were clinging to hate, judgment, or some other thing that made them remain closed-off. It was of their own free will. There were only a small multitude of these darker spheres among the huge multitudes of us who shone with the bright Light of God.

Their hearts may have been embittered to the extent they would not receive love even when it was offered unconditionally. I thought I recognized at least one of the faces. I thought to myself, "it truly is hell to be cut-off from the Light." The darker spheres were indifferent toward the love and light of the Creator. I wondered how anyone could be indifferent to that Love. Perhaps it was their lack of faith, belief, and trust in God that caused them to be separate, unable to see, know, or understand that God was right there with them.

Isn't that how it is on earth as well? We deny, avoid, and turn our backs on God and each other, until our lives are wretched and dark? And is this not our training ground to know, accept, and trust God, so that when we are home with Him in Heaven, He will acknowledge us as we acknowledge Him?

If We Go to Heaven, From Where Do We Come?

Of the memories I have been allowed to keep of the crossing, nothing amazed me more than the creation of new souls. The I Am simply spoke, and they were born out of the Creator, and sent streaking through the gray mist surrounding the celestial realm. The souls pierced the mist, and passed into earth life where a new body-self and mind-self awaited its soul. Thousands of times the Creator spoke these souls into being, pronouncing "Become now Taylor Wynn Layman" and – pop – zip – off went Taylor Wynn through the mist, and into this world.

Why does the Creator continue to make new souls? I had the answers to this and other philosophical questions as if they were second grade material. However, it was an answer I lost in the return back to this life. Just know that we are spoken into creation with great love and great power. All of heaven resounded with your creation, and waits to welcome you home when you are done walking your path.

What Do We Do for All of Eternity?

I remember when I was young, how very boring I thought heaven would be. Who would want to sit in an eternal church service? Who would want to sing praises all day long? Sorry, but at twenty-one, you don't find that an inspiring picture. I never heard a sermon about what we did in heaven for eternity. I think there is a good reason for not hearing one. They simply didn't know how to convey it.

Let's try an earthly version of heaven…

Think of times in your life, perhaps a moment you felt nothing could go wrong—the world was your oyster! You landed the high-paying job, got the posh office, the most beautiful girl you know agreed to go on a date with you in the prize Ferrari you just received from your boss as a bonus! You drive the Ferrari to your yacht, and kick your feet up as you watch the gulls sweep by against the blue sky. You dial in Pachelbel's Canon in D on the radio, and sip your pina colada. She sits beside you in her tropical dress, as your friends pass and make hissing sounds because, baby, you've got it all going for you! Everything is surreal—you motor around a bit, and come to rest at a waterfall. There is a cave revealing itself from either side of the rushing stream of falling water.

From under the falls, and peeping just around the corner, is a winged being who bids you come and rest in the cave. Pachelbel's Canon continues to play, though you are now several yards from the radio. Your head feels lighter as you watch the winged being prepare a bed of soft branches and moss just for your resting pleasure. Everything has been attended to—everything is right. This is a heaven-on-earth scene designed to help you "feel" a miniature experience of the ecstasy you will feel in heaven.

Now, take that good "earth feeling" to the infinite level. Yes, Heaven is that good! Being in the company of the Creator brings feelings of elation, rapture, and ecstasy. It is the celebration of being in a total state of love, peace, power, and acceptance.

Imagine how wonderful it feels! There is no pain, no limits of the body; there is no limit to your knowledge, or your ability to connect with one another. There is nothing boring about Heaven!

I long to be there again. There are endless people to meet, endless love to experience, endless peace to enjoy, and endless grace spilling-out from the Creator. It is the feeling of being at Home. Oh, how I miss it!

Closing Remarks

It has been a true spiritual blessing to share my crossing over experiences with you. In sharing, we learn to heal others and ourselves. If you enjoyed this book, you might also enjoy my book, **Spirit Thinking**: *Your 30 Day Guide to Enlightenment.* It is a workbook that will teach you how to apply the qualities of the Source, discovered during my crossing, to your life, right here and right now. Get your copy online at **www.SpiritThinking.Net**, or ask for it at your favorite bookstore. Learn what I learned about healing with help from the Source. I believe healing must first come from a Spirit level of Truth—with a capital T.

I continue to battle my chronic pain. The neuropathic pain becomes so bad that at times I have to simply put my feet up and weep. But I find myself more and more patient with all things, including the pain.

If you are in chronic pain, know that God loves you, and is not trying to punish you. Know that you are in good company with the Master, Jesus, and saints like St.Paul, St.Teresa, St. Francis, and more recent icons like Padre Pio, and Mother Theresa, who suffered through various types of maladies, and continued to serve the Lord patiently, boldly, and wisely. Truly, your rewards are in heaven!

If you have a question about NDEs, the afterlife, or if you need counseling, you may write to me at ***reece@manley.net***. Who knows, I might include your question in my next book (with your permission.)

In closing, I want all to know that I am glad to be back here in this time and place to be blessed by the wonderful people around me. Heaven waits for all of us, but we must also wait for Heaven! Until then, we all have work to do to fulfill our individual journeys. I hope your journey is going well here in this life.

Remember, you are a blessing, created by God, and spoken into being by your loving Creator. Your destiny is love, compassion, peace, and yes, power—power to change that which needs changing. May your path lead you to treat yourself and others with greater compassion, support, kindness, and LOVE—against which there is no law.

With all blessings,

Reece

Acknowledgements

I would like to express my deep and sincere appreciation to my dear colleague and friend, Dr. Freda Chaney. Freda is a person beyond compare in her intuition, insight, and generosity. This work would not have been possible without her kindness, guiding hand, and intelligent editing. My appreciation, dear Freda.

I again would like to acknowledge my family for their patience and support during the time of this work. Dad, Mom, Ross, Kerryann, Rian, and Rory all spent time without me so I might spend time with you.

Of course, my deepest gratitude goes to our Creator, Whose wisdom is contained within, and Who led you to pick up this book.

Advocate USA Publishing

A division of Advocate USA

www.ingramcontent.com/pod-product-compliance
Lightning Source LLC
Chambersburg PA
CBHW080543170426
43195CB00016B/2661